PINHEADS AND PATRIOTS

PINHEADS
AND PATRIOTS

Where You Stand in the Age of Obama

Bill O'Reilly

WILLIAM MORROW
An Imprint of HarperCollinsPublishers

HarperCollins books may be purchased for educational, business, or sales promotional use. For information please write: Special Markets Department, HarperCollins Publishers, 10 East 53rd Street, New York, NY 10022.

FIRST EDITION

Library of Congress Cataloging-in-Publication Data

O'Reilly, Bill.
  Pinheads and patriots : where you stand in the age of Obama / Bill O'Reilly. — 1st ed.
    p. cm.
  Includes index.
  ISBN 978-0-06-195071-1 (hardcover)
  1. United States—Politics and government—2009– 2. Obama, Barack. I. Title.
  E907.R74 2010
  973.932—dc22

2010027958

10 11 12 13 14   OV/RRD   10 9 8 7 6 5 4 3 2 1

This book is dedicated to Madeline and Spencer.
Kids do not come any better.

ACKNOWLEDGMENTS

The following people helped immensely in putting this book together. Crack editors Charles Flowers and Hope Innelli. Agent extraordinaire Eric Simonoff. And the best assistant on the earth, Makeda Wubneh.

CONTENTS

★

PINHEADS AND PATRIOTS

This One's for You

HEY, YOU! YOU, THE AMERICAN! You who believe in life, liberty, and the pursuit of happiness. This book is about you. No spin.

In this age of Obama, all that you take for granted is changing, yet many Americans have no clue. So I've decided to fix that. After reading the following pages, you will know precisely what's going on in the United States. Then you can plan exactly how to deal with the massive shift in the way our country is being run. Trust me, you need to know what is really happening so that you can make effective decisions for yourself.

These changes are not all bad, but they're not all good, either. Many will hurt you and your family. Most media people and politicians won't tell you that because they don't care about you. But I do.

Why? It's very simple: you guys have made me rich and famous. I worked hard to position myself to succeed, but you made it happen.

Without you watching me on TV and reading my books, I would be just another energetic bloviator—perhaps teaching school in Miami or reporting the news in Dallas. I appreciate the fact that millions of you have contributed to my success, so now it's payback time: I will vividly chronicle the changes occurring in an America that your great-grandparents would never recognize today, because knowing the facts is how you can preserve the things you love about this country most—the things they loved, too.

As you must know by now, it has been a great adventure for me to write five consecutive bestselling nonfiction books over the years, and again, I'm grateful that you were there right along with me on those adventures.

My previous book, *A Bold Fresh Piece of Humanity*, was considered my most personal to date. It is about how my life overlapped with your life and how my upbringing and experiences brought me to a place where I can speak to millions of folks every day. We had a lot of fun in *Bold* and we'll have some laughs in *P & P*, too, but this effort is completely different. Again, this book is about *your* life in America. And there is no more important time to talk about you than right now.

As you may know, each episode of my TV program, *The O'Reilly Factor,* ends with a segment called "Pinheads and Patriots," in which I call out both people who are doing good things (Patriots), and those who are doing awful, dumb, or evil things (Pinheads). Although the expositions range from the banal (dealing with Snoop Dogg) to the deadly serious (addressing the actions of world leaders), they are always about influencers—individuals whose actions, good or bad, affect you. Research shows that this segment has become a hit with the *Factor* audience for this very reason.

To break it down so that even Nancy Pelosi can understand it, there are basically two kinds of people in the world: those whose thoughts and actions say "me first," and those whose primary goal is to look out for others the same way they would look out for themselves (a Judeo-Christian philosophy). Generally speaking, the Patriots come from the second category.

Sure, it's true that most of us are self-centered, at least some of the time. But how we deal with that reality defines whether we are a Pinhead or a Patriot. As always, free will prevails.

Sometimes, the evaluation of these people's actions gets complicated. For example, President John F. Kennedy did some great things for poor Americans, and he also handled the Russian threat in Cuba with admirable courage. But JFK was also needlessly ruthless at times and used people in deceitful ways. So the President was both a Pinhead and a Patriot. As you can see, defining his short life in consistent terms is very difficult to do because he was capable of both extraordinary good and incredible callousness.

Similarly, President George W. Bush is a challenge to define. He did a number of truly noble things, especially during his first term. His ferocity against murderous members of al-Qaeda likely saved thousands of American lives. His generosity in fighting disease in Africa also saved millions of lives, and that important humanitarian work continues to this day.

Unfortunately, the Pinhead factor exists for him as well, because the Iraq War was not only poorly planned but most likely unnecessary. Also, Mr. Bush's failure to aggressively oversee the economy led to rampant speculation and financial con games galore. The results were obviously catastrophic; the recession damaged the lives of countless people all over the world.

But this book is not about past Presidents per se.

In fact, much of it will be devoted to discussing the present occupant of the Oval Office. President Barack Obama is, perhaps, the most polarizing chief executive since Abraham Lincoln. Yes, opinions about Bill Clinton and Bush the Younger divided the country, but not in the way views about Mr. Obama have. Some Americans sincerely believe he is trying to change the fundamental core of the United States. You hear this critical refrain all the time: "When do I get my country back?"

The Obama factor is, of course, fluid. It is being played out every day in thousands of ways. For this reason, it is imperative that you, the loyal American, continue to watch and understand its impact on *your* place in America. Thus, the subtitle of this book—*Where You Stand in the Age of Obama*—and my mandate to take a hard look at the President.

On June 9, 2010, the world's most influential newspaper, the *Wall Street Journal,* printed an op-ed piece by Dorothy Rabinowitz, a member of the paper's editorial board.

The article, entitled "The Alien in the White House," made a devastating case that Barack Obama has little in common with working, everyday Americans. Ms. Rabinowitz put forth the view that the President simply has no understanding of you and your life. As a result, his leadership is based on theory, not reality. She also asserted that Americans are beginning to notice the emotional distance between them and their leader.

The op-ed was provocative and damaging to the President, especially in the midst of a brutal economy and the oil spill catastrophe in the Gulf of Mexico. The polls show Mr. Obama losing the support of independent voters and even some liberal voters. Is the President detached from your reality? Is he a man who lives primarily within himself? We will try to answer those questions in the following pages.

But this much can be said with absolute certainty about *all* national leaders: sometimes they are Pinheads and sometimes they are Patriots, as we cited with the examples of JFK and W. But when the stakes are as high as they are right now in America—with historical debt and a war against crazy Islamic jihadists, some of whom are seeking nuclear weapons—leadership becomes amazingly important. Let's be blunt: a Pinhead making a national security mistake could very well get thousands of Americans killed. And a continuation of out-of-control spending could shatter the entire economy.

Therefore, I have a responsibility to provide you, the reader, with an honest appraisal of your situation in this age of Obama. I can't embrace ideology, myth, or propaganda. I've got to cut through the fog and define whether socialism, corruption, incompetence, and yes, even evil are in the air.

So determining the roster of Pinheads and Patriots is a complicated business, as you can see, and I do not make these designations lightly. Nobody's perfect, but, in most cases, a pattern of behavior does emerge. And we'll be looking for the pattern together in this book. To get us started, I have two clear examples of how I determine P&P status: say hello to Congressman Barney Frank, and please consider the late Tony Snow.

★

CHAPTER 1

Essential Examples of a Pinhead and a Patriot

LET'S BEGIN WITH THE DEFINITION of *Pinhead* as put forth in the book *A Dictionary of Slang and Unconventional English*, compiled by Eric Partridge. "Pinhead—A simple fellow, a fool. So small a head can contain but few brains."

Then there's the definition that Urban Dictionary drops on us: "One who lacks the intelligence of the 'normal' sector of the human population; [one who] cannot handle the most mundane tasks due to lack of common sense and intelligence."

And, finally, it may be worth noting that popular music spells the meaning out as D-U-M-B. Just listen to the lyrics of punk rocker Dee Dee Ramone's popular song "Pinhead" to see what I mean.

I'm also aware that there is a song called "Pinheads Are Every-where" by Dan Hiatt and No Sisters, but since I already know that

Pinheads are everywhere and I have written this book to prove it, I have not sought out that song.

Obviously, my personal definition of a Pinhead is much broader than the slang term implies. Some very intelligent people can be Pinheads and often are. It applies to individual actions. As you will read, you can be a Pinhead one day and a Patriot the next. But Pinhead status is a slippery slope. Get in with the wrong crowd, get taken by your own success, or get some bad advice, and all of that can lead to residence in Pinheadville, a place you should avoid if you can.

On the Patriot front the definition is a lot easier. I like this description of Patriotism by Adlai Stevenson, the liberal politician who ran for President twice against Dwight Eisenhower and got his butt kicked both times: "Patriotism is not short, frenzied outbursts of emotion, but the tranquil and steady dedication of a lifetime."

Throughout my life, I've been fortunate enough to know many American Patriots. For our purposes here, let's spotlight one you might well remember.

COURAGE IN THE FACE OF ADVERSITY

My friend Tony Snow was the bravest man I ever met. When he died of cancer in July 2008, I was not surprised. I had watched him fight the insidious disease for years. He was my colleague at Fox News and later, of course, the chief spokesman for the Bush White House.

As you may know, I called him "Snow," and we energetically debated public policy on both radio and TV. Even though I was angrier about stuff than he was a lot of the time, our philosophies were similar, with the exception of party politics—he was a committed Republican; I am a registered Independent.

Because we had good on-air chemistry, Westwood One signed Tony as my primary substitute for *The Radio Factor*. The guy was brilliant, honest, and really cared about the welfare of his country. Snow was a better man than I am. He was a guy to emulate.

Born in Berea, Kentucky, on June 1, 1955, Tony Snow was raised in a working-class community in the Cincinnati area. After graduating from Davidson College and continuing his studies at the University of Chicago, Snow took a journalism job in Greensboro, North Carolina, in 1979 and worked his way up from there to national prominence.

He did what I did. He started small and ultimately made it big.

In April 2006 President Bush selected Tony Snow to replace Scott McClellan as the primary White House spokesperson. He was great at it—disarming the partisan Left press corps with quips and good-natured teasing. But all the while, Snow was fighting a disease that relentlessly attacked his colon.

Before he took the political job, he ran it by me, weighing the pros and cons. I told him this: "Snow, you will have a window to the world that few other human beings ever have. You believe Bush is a force for good, and you can help him. So you have no choice—you have to take the job."

He did, of course. And truthfully, I could hear in his voice that he had made that decision even before we finished our conversation.

But by the summer of 2007, I sensed Snow was having a tough time with the cancer treatments, and I feared he would not make it. He never said that, but I knew he felt his situation was precarious. Even then, his primary motivation was not for his own well-being. It was for that of others. He was concerned about his wife, Jill, and his three children. He wanted to protect their financial futures, so, knowing that the end was coming, Tony resigned from the White House in September 2007 and used his last days to make money in the private sector. Racing against time, he took as many paid speaking engagements as he could. I watched as he flew around the country, all the while suffering tremendous pain. It was heartbreaking, but Snow never once complained.

When we spoke, I'd always begin with the question: "Snow, how you doing?"

He always replied, "I'm doing great!" But he wasn't.

His funeral was held at Washington's National Cathedral on Thursday, July 17, 2008. It was a beautiful day, and the Catholic ceremony was packed with many of the country's most powerful people, including President and Mrs. Bush and Vice President and Mrs. Cheney. Tony's family sat in the first pew in front of the altar. I was one row behind them on the right, flanked by a number of my Fox News colleagues.

After receiving communion, I was able to squeeze Jill Snow's hand. It was all I could do. Everything had been said in the days before Tony's death. I saw the President, and he nodded at me. Again, what more could be said?

The *Washington Post* covered Tony Snow's funeral with dignity. The *New York Times* ignored it. Just thought you'd like to know that.

Patriot and former White House Press Secretary Tony Snow waves good-bye as he departs the White House on his final day at the office.

As the years go by, Tony Snow will be remembered by his friends as a great man and as a Patriot. There is no higher accolade on this planet. Tony was just fifty-three when he died.

THE COWARDLY LION

Now let's head over to Pinheadville, a place where I assign folks if they do something extremely stupid, or wind up damaging other people by their actions. As we've discussed before, being a Pinhead does not have to be a lifelong designation. There is always the prospect of redemption for Pinheads if the dopey stuff stops. Sometimes someone can be both a Patriot and a Pinhead in a short period of time. But for our purposes here, it is important to define clearly what a Pinhead is. And for that we turn to the vivid example of my pal Congressman Barney Frank.

After serving almost thirty years in the House of Representatives, Barney Frank has earned some Patriotic credentials, no doubt about it. The Massachusetts liberal is a force in Congress, and you have to give him credit for his public service. But after that, things get murky, and the dreaded Pinhead label comes into play.

As chairman of the House Financial Services Committee, Frank had a front-row seat from which to watch the economy collapse. Even worse, Barney directly oversaw the two federal mortgage houses, Fannie Mae and Freddie Mac, which were so poorly run they made Somalia look like Switzerland.

But if you ask Frank about any of this, as I did, you get outrageous spin and blatant denials of any fault. According to Barney, *he* was a victim of the economic chaos. None of it had anything to do with him. He's quick to say that Bush did it or to offer some other lame defense.

So let's look at the record to see whether or not Frank falls into the Pinhead category.

On July 14, 2008, less than two months before the American public became aware that the economy was headed south fast, Barney Frank said this on CNBC:

I think this is a case where Fannie and Freddie are fundamentally sound, that they are not in danger of going under. They're not the best investments these days from the long-term standpoint going back. [But] I think they are in good shape going forward . . . their prospects going forward are very solid.

Clear and straightforward, right? The top guy overseeing Fannie and Freddie is sounding the all-clear down the road. Good news!

Well, as you know, two months later Fannie, Freddie, and the entire American housing industry tanked. The reason: bad loans made by both government and private banks. Frank was clueless, even though he was in a position of oversight. The folks were depending on him to protect them from financial fools. Frank let us down.

But instead of admitting his appalling mistake and apologizing to those who may have invested in Fannie and Freddie because of him, Barney came on the *Factor* and lied. On October 2, 2008, I ran the CNBC clip and then confronted the congressman:

Bill O'Reilly: Shouldn't everybody in the country be angry with you right now?

Barney Frank: No. You've misrepresented this consistently. I became chairman of the [finance] committee on January 31, 2007. Less than two months later, I did what the Republicans hadn't been able to do in twelve years—get through the committee a very tough regulatory bill. And it passed the House in May. I've always said two things about Fannie Mae and Freddie Mac, that they have an important role to play, but that regulations need to be improved.

O'Reilly: That's swell, but you still went out in July and said everything was great. And off that, a lot of people bought stock and have lost everything they had.

Frank: Oh, no.

O'Reilly [*voice rising*]: Oh, yes!

Frank: I said it wasn't a good investment.

O'Reilly: Don't give me any of that. We just heard your own words. You want me to play them again for you?

Frank: You didn't listen to it. . . . I said it wasn't a good investment.

O'Reilly: You said going forward it was going to be swell. . . . Let's stop the crap, stop the BS.

Frank: You know, that's the problem with your show.

O'Reilly: Under your tutelage the [housing] industry has declined 90 percent.

Frank: Yes, but—

O'Reilly: And none of this was your fault? Oh, no. People lost millions of dollars, but it wasn't your fault? Come on, you coward, say the truth.

Frank: What do you mean, "coward"?

O'Reilly: You're a coward. You blame everybody else.

Frank: Bill, here's the problem with your show. You start ranting and the only way to respond is almost to look as boorish as you. But here are the facts. I specifically said in the quote you just played that I didn't think it was a good investment. I wasn't telling anybody to buy stock. Secondly, I wasn't presiding idly over this. I was trying to get regulations adopted.

O'Reilly: Bottom line is, the stock [Fannie Mae] drops 90 percent.

Frank: Yes.

O'Reilly: In any private industry, you're out.

Frank: No.

O'Reilly: But not in the federal government. You can come in here and make every excuse in the world.

Frank: I'm not going to be bullied by your ranting. You can rant all you want, you're not going to shut me up! The problem was, we passed a bill in 1994—

O'Reilly: Now we're back to 1994. This is bull. This is why Americans don't trust their government.

Frank: No, this is why your stupidity gets in the way of rational discussion.

The shoot-out went on for a few more minutes, but you get the picture. Barney Frank, who had a clear window to the banking industry's effect on the economy, warned no one that the loan situation was out of control. Why? *Because he didn't know.* What he said on CNBC was pathetically true. He thought things would be fine "going forward."

Now, there's nothing wrong with making an honest mistake. But when our elected leaders will not admit their failings and they play the blame game instead, you, the loyal American, get hurt two times over. First, the pols screw up whatever policy they're associated with. Then, they deceive those who have been hammered by their ineptitude with lame excuses designed to avoid accountability. Not acceptable.

Barney Frank can bamboozle most interviewers. Not this one. Based on the facts, Frank played a major role in the collapse of the mortgage market. The fact that he won't admit that makes him a classic Pinhead.

Any questions?

House Financial Services Committee Chairman Barney Frank (D-MA) wonders what went wrong at a July 2008 committee hearing on the state of the economy.

In May 2010 a ridiculous footnote was added to the Barney saga. Congress passed new financial oversight legislation. Guess who was out front telling Americans that the tough new law would protect us from further shenanigans in the money industry? Hey, Barney, this Bud's for you. It was unbelievable.

CHAPTER 2

Barack Hussein Obama—
Who Exactly Is This Guy?

MY COLLEAGUE GLENN BECK thinks that the forty-fourth President of the United States is a subversive, a man bent on changing America into some kind of socialistic nanny state that might, God help us, actually resemble France. Beck passionately believes that Barack Obama is a danger to everything Beck values. So Glenn has moved aggressively to challenge the President by using his daily radio and television programs to illustrate the radical stuff he believes is being promoted by the Obama administration.

Rush Limbaugh and many other conservative radio commentators believe pretty much the same thing: that the President is a force for pernicious change, a committed socialist in a two-thousand-dollar suit.

These guys pound President Obama into pudding just about every day, and millions of Americans are spooning up the dessert.

But I'm not so sure this scorched-earth strategy aimed at the President is good for the country. I favor a more surgical approach.

Yes, Mr. Obama can be a Pinhead, as we will illustrate, but all Presidents, as I stated, can be assigned a place in that category from time to time. Exactly what Barack Obama's big-picture vision is remains to be seen. It is entirely possible he doesn't even have a big-picture scenario. It seems to me that the President is certainly a committed left-wing guy who thrives on power and attention, but I don't see him as Karl Marx reincarnated.

I could be wrong.

T-shirts bearing slogans popularized by Glenn Beck in his fight against President Obama's perceived socialism are a hot commodity these days.

Whenever a journalist like me tries to define a President, the situation gets complicated. Accurate analysis is challenging because outsiders (that's us) can never get all the facts about what goes on in the Oval Office. I mean, I get interesting intelligence information because of my visibility on the *Factor,* but confirming the validity of it is simply impossible. In other words, I hear and see things, but sometimes context is elusive. Why did Obama do that? How could he have hired this guy? Those are questions that are often asked but rarely answered.

It is soooooo boring to hear Obama supporters bleating out approval no matter what the President does. And it is equally dull to hear the man bashed even for getting up in the morning. That kind of blind partisanship does you no good at all. The good news is, dishonest media like the *New York Times* and MSNBC are failing. People are simply walking away. The United States needs tough, fair reporting about President Obama because the man's vision for the country is so different from what he put forth during the campaign. Back in 2008 when Obama was still a senator, he was on the moderate Left. He was a guy who sought reform but not radical change. Since becoming President, however, Obama has emerged as a crusader for "social justice" and has rejected unilateralism overseas. His record spending and softer approach on jihad (he won't even say the word) have caused deep angst in many quarters. But there is definitely a method to the President's alleged madness, a central reason for what he is putting out there. A core mission of this book is to define that reason and put a Pinhead or Patriot label on it.

By the book's end, you'll have a pretty good idea into which category the President belongs. But be forewarned—while we will be brutally honest, we will also be totally fair to the man. It would not be Patriotic to cheap-shot the commander in chief, especially because he's already staked out some solid positions. Two quick examples are as follows:

Speaking at a Town Hall meeting in the East Room at the White House on Father's Day 2009, the President said this to American men who father children and leave them:

*Just because your own father wasn't there for you, that's
not an excuse for you to be absent, also—it's all the more
reason for you to be present.*

*You have an obligation to break the cycle and learn from
those mistakes, and to rise up where your own fathers fell
short and to do better than they did with your own children.*

That statement is not exactly breaking news, but it is correct and
badly needed advice in a country where 17 million children are living with their mothers in single-parent households.

The second example of the President taking a strong and necessary stand occurred on June 6, 2009, at the Esperanza National Hispanic Prayer Breakfast and Conference, where the President directly
addressed the illegal immigration mess:

*The American people believe in immigration, but they
also believe that we can't tolerate a situation where people
come to the United States in violation of the law. . . .*

*For those who wish to become citizens, we should require
them to pay a penalty and pay taxes, learn English, go to the
back of the line behind those who play by the rules.*

In this latter instance, the words are all there, but the deeds may
be lacking. At this point in history, the border with Mexico is becoming more secure thanks to the incredibly expensive barrier fence and
increased federal patrolling that have been put in place. But as the
controversial Arizona law allowing state and local police to detain
suspected illegal aliens who are already involved in a police matter
demonstrates, the border/alien problem is still a mess, and the federal government must stop the madness or the states themselves will
take action.

BORDERLINE PINHEADS

As you may know, the *Factor* editorialized as far back as the year 2002 that the National Guard be deployed to back up the patrol efforts. President Bush resisted that for years but did, after a series of grisly crimes in the area, finally order about 5,000 guardsmen to the border. Wherever they were stationed, crime and smuggling dropped big-time. I mean, come on, if you're a drug or people smuggler and you know there's a chance of running into the U.S. military, are you going to take the risk of being captured and having your illegal cargo seized? Not likely.

After Mr. Bush left office, the Obama administration pulled the National Guard back. Why? I don't know. No explanation was forthcoming. But then Arizona went wild, and on May 26, 2010, the President finally ordered a small contingent of the guard to return. The announcement said "up to 1,200" troops would be deployed. But that is far too few, is it not?

In making the National Guard announcement, President Obama, like President Bush before him, seemed reluctant. Clearly, his heart was not into having a military presence there.

U.S. Border Patrol agents (pictured here in Sasabe, Arizona) need more help from the National Guard to deal with the influx of illegal aliens.

But why not? The answer has to be politics. Both Obama and Bush believe that many Hispanic Americans resent immigration actions that target their brothers and sisters. And Hispanics are a fast-growing voting bloc, one that gave Barack Obama much support.

So when the President saw his job favorability rating drop 12 points in the first four months of 2010, giant red flags went up. That's why Mr. Obama will not take dramatic action to seal the border with Mexico even though narcotics and illegal aliens continue to flow into the United States.

On the Republican side, the Grand Old Party needs to win back at least some Hispanic support. President Bush understood the importance of wooing the socially conservative Hispanic voting bloc and did everything he could to mollify that group, including looking the other way as millions of illegal aliens crossed into the United States. President Obama has continued Bush's policy.

But the rest of America isn't buying it. Polls say that the majority of American voters support a tough crackdown on the illegal alien intrusion (about 60 percent approved of the Arizona law). President Obama sided with the Far Left, however, and condemned the Arizona legislature, explaining that he believes the Arizona authorities might practice "racial profiling" in enforcing the law. That, of course, is speculation, but the President has fully embraced the anti-Arizona point of view and ordered the Justice Department to sue the state—a boneheaded political move if there ever was one. The President and his lawyers apparently believe that states are prohibited from passing laws dealing with immigration enforcement because that is the sole responsibility of the federal government. In fact, just as this book was going to print, and hours before the new immigration law was to go into effect, one of Arizona's own courts, under U.S. District Court Judge Susan Bolton, sided with the Justice Department's position, placing an injunction on provisions of the law stating that they "would impose a 'distinct, unusual, and extraordinary' burden on legal resident aliens that only the federal government has the authority to impose." This is the crux of the Obama lawsuit.

Fox News anchor and attorney Megyn Kelly believes that there is legal precedent for allowing Arizona to better protect itself against the invasion it is experiencing. But Ms. Kelly also points out that the lawsuit is heavily ideological and federal judges are likely to rule on what they believe, not what the Constitution says and what previous courts have upheld. Like the *Bush v. Gore* case, which was decided in the Supreme Court along ideological lines, this lawsuit will most likely produce an obviously partisan split. But just the fact that President Obama is once again at odds with the American people makes the story extremely important and compelling.

Realizing that he was lining up against the will of most Americans, Mr. Obama knew he had to do *something,* so he pulled out the National Guard card and gently put it on the table. As stated before, though, his heart isn't into sending the guardsmen there, no matter how small the number.

The blunt truth is that both President Obama and President Bush are Pinheads when it comes to securing the southern border of the United States. The federal government's primary constitutional responsibility is to protect the rights of Americans and keep them safe from foreign intrusion. Certainly, more than 10 million illegal aliens running around the country basically unsupervised is an intrusion. Ten thousand guardsmen stationed on the border would dramatically reduce the smuggling of drugs and human beings into our homeland. The soldiers would protect American citizens under siege down there and would prevent the brutal exploitation of the aliens themselves. It is flat-out disgraceful that the U.S. border with Mexico has been a sieve for decades. There is absolutely no excuse for that other than a lack of will on the part of our Presidents.

Sooner or later, a tough but fair assessment of illegal aliens already in the USA is going to happen, but nothing will be accomplished on that front until Americans are convinced that the border is under control. That could be a major problem for Mr. Obama going forward. Like President Bush before him, Obama seems squeamish on border security. Even taking into account the Hispanic American vote, I could never understand why our leaders simply will not do the right thing for the country. It's insane. Allowing illegal alien chaos is one of the biggest Pinhead policies ever designed, and the vast majority of the American people, including Hispanics, know it. Our prisons are full of aliens who have committed violent crimes against Americans. Just that awful fact alone should compel a strict illegal alien policy. So the President is caught between Barack and a hard place on this one. Yes, he's his own biggest obstacle here. He's playing to his Far Left base, who essentially want open borders. In the meantime, the majority of the American people want security and order. Along with national health care (which illegal aliens will receive, you watch), the immigration issue could wind up badly damaging Mr. Obama's political future.

WHEN EVERYTHING STARTED TO TANK

In addition to having their ideology and hypothetical wish lists tested, all Presidents have to contend with the problem-solving factor. And it is here that Barack Obama took a terrible beating in the spring of 2010—a hammering that might limit him to one term in office.

On April 20 a British Petroleum deepwater oil rig exploded and sank one mile to the bottom of the Gulf of Mexico. In the disaster, which took place forty-two miles off the coast of Louisiana, eleven workers were killed. Two days after the explosion destroyed the $560 million Horizon rig, a five-mile-long oil slick was sighted. BP announced that the equivalent of about 1,000 barrels of oil a day was seeping into the Gulf, but the company confidently stated it would soon have things under control. Sure. I don't know about you, but I was skeptical from the jump about BP's honesty. Also, I knew damn well that the federal government was counting on the oil company to fix the problem, and in life, whenever you count on someone else you're often disappointed. By the way, about those 1,000 barrels a day? The true number was more than eight times that, and there has since been documentation suggesting that the number could be as high as 100,000 barrels a day!

Five days after the explosion, the U.S. Coast Guard approved various plans to cap the leak. Four days after that, with the oil still gushing 24/7 in front of underwater cameras, President Obama finally began visibly taking charge. He ordered a variety of federal agencies to take action, mostly exploratory, and sternly told the world that the United States would hold BP completely responsible.

By early June, with the oil pollution still out of control, the President was under siege. Front-page photos of birds covered with oil, along with scores of TV interviews with folks losing their jobs, brought the situation to a boil. A Quinnipiac poll found that 59 percent of Americans believed Mr. Obama was handling the situation poorly. The liberal media, which had pounded President Bush quickly and unmercifully for slow action after Hurricane Katrina, were finally forced to scrutinize Obama's reaction to the BP disaster. Things got bloody fast. Speaking on *Good Morning America*, Democratic pundit James Carville shook up the liberal world when he said:

> *The President of the United States could have come down here. He could have been involved with the families of these eleven people [who died]. He could have commandeered . . . research vessels in the Gulf of Mexico.*
>
> *These people [living on the Gulf Coast] are crying, they're begging for something down here. And it just looks like he's not involved in this. Man, you got to get down here and take control of this. Put somebody in charge of this thing and get this thing moving. We're about to die down here.*

President Barack Obama arrives in Venice, Louisiana, twelve days after the region was affected by the BP oil spill. He's seen here greeting Coast Guard first responders.

The committed Left was stunned. Carville going after Obama? Then things got even worse. While most of her fellow *New York Times* columnists continued to make excuses for President Obama, Maureen Dowd wrote the following:

> *Too often it feels as though Barry [Obama's childhood name] is watching from a balcony, reluctant to enter the fray until the clamor of the crowd forces him to come down. The pattern is perverse. The man whose presidency is rooted in his ability to inspire withholds that inspiration when it is most needed.*

Wow. Remember, those comments were from *liberals!*

The right-wing media, of course, went wild. As you might expect, talk radio covered itself in oil. Conservative partisans, angrily remembering the Bush-Katrina media coverage, hit hard. Right-wing intellectuals, some of whom were not Obama-bashers, predicted doom for the President. Writing in the *Wall Street Journal*, columnist Peggy Noonan summed up that point of view:

> *The disaster in the Gulf may well spell the political end of the President and his administration. . . . It's not good to have a President in this position—weakened, polarizing and lacking broad public support—less than halfway through his term.*

From my perch on television, I clearly observed the "nuts-r-us" brigades swinging into action. On the Far Left, the loons began blaming Bush and Cheney for the spill. On the Far Right, there were cries of conspiracy, the theory being that the President intentionally let the disaster get out of control so that he could damage the oil companies beyond repair.

So what is the truth here? Well, like many things, it's complicated. No President could have prevented that oil spill. Deep-well offshore drilling is here to stay, and obviously there is risk involved. Realizing almost immediately that he had no solutions to the spill and staggering pollution, Mr. Obama gambled and allowed BP to take the lead. That decision cost the President valuable time, as BP failed dismally to stop the leak or prevent the rapidly spreading oil from staining mainland America.

The governor of Louisiana, Bobby Jindal, watched all this with horror. Early on, his people had wanted the federal government to approve a massive sand barrier installation project to protect Louisiana's vital wetlands. But the feds dithered, citing environmental concerns. And that was legitimate. If you build a barrier in front of wetlands, there will be unintended consequences. The Army Corps of Engineers knows that, so there was big-time tension between the feds and the state of Louisiana.

What makes the situation even more fascinating is that exactly the same thing happened after Hurricane Katrina slammed New Orleans. The state was telling the feds to do one thing, but the Bush administration had other ideas. It was chaos. And the press harpooned Mr. Bush.

Would those oil-blocking barriers that Governor Jindal wanted have worked? Nobody knows. But once again, the American people were subjected to watching a terrible disaster career out of control on the Gulf Coast. I mean, it was eerie. President Bush lost a ton of credibility after Hurricane Katrina's force caused massive and visible human suffering for weeks, and now the identical thing was happening to President Obama, who, by the way, had hammered Bush over Katrina while campaigning for the presidency. As I've said, karma can be a bitch and make anyone look like a Pinhead, even though the press generally gave Mr. Obama an easier time than they did with George W. Bush.

At the moment, it is impossible to assess exactly how much the oil disaster has hurt the President. But it is clear that his credibility as a problem-solver was gravely damaged. Also, as political heat generated by the oil slick rose, the President's famously cool demeanor raised questions once again about his leadership style. In times of crisis, "slick" doesn't usually cut it. Pardon the pun.

THE PEACE SURPRIZE

At this point it may be worth taking a deep breath to clear our heads and change direction. Let's be fair and define some of Mr. Obama's Patriotic credentials. They begin on the personal side of his life. The rise of Barack Obama has been well chronicled and is truly an amazing story. Both Mr. Obama and Bill Clinton have demonstrated that humble beginnings can motivate people to accomplish just about anything. In Obama's case, his achievement is even more astonishing, since his upbringing without a father was extremely chaotic.

Although that story has already been told, it warrants mention again as it is, indeed, a Patriotic one. Only in America, I believe, can a boy as disadvantaged as Barry Obama once was grow up to become the leader of a great nation.

However, the question going forward is this: Will the man Barack Obama has become achieve greatness with the opportunity the voters have given him? Right now the tea leaves (some covered with oil) seem to be saying no, but the President does have substantial time left in office.

What else are those tea leaves saying? Let's begin our microanalysis of Obama's fortunes with the Nobel Peace Prize. On October 9, 2009, the Norwegian Nobel Committee, consisting of five guys wearing heavy woolen sweaters, announced that the President had won the prestigious award that carries with it a $1.4 million cash prize.

The Nobel Committee chairman, Thorbjørn Jagland (Thorby for short), told the world that the President won for "extraordinary efforts to strengthen international diplomacy and cooperation between peoples."

Thorby, the former prime minister of Norway, went on to explain that Mr. Obama's desire to reduce the world's stock of nuclear arms had also impressed the committee.

The President himself was caught off guard. After deliberating for a few hours, he said this about the peace prize:

> *Let me be clear: I do not view it as a recognition of*
> *my own accomplishments, but rather as an affirmation of*
> *American leadership on behalf of aspirations held by people*
> *in all nations. To be honest, I do not feel that I deserve to be in*
> *the company of so many of the transformative figures who've*
> *been honored by this prize.*

That would be folks like Jimmy Carter, Al Gore, and Yasser Arafat, to name a few—the latter of whom, you will remember, amassed millions of dollars by siphoning off foreign aid intended for the beleaguered Palestinian people. Wouldn't you have loved to witness old Yasser's face when that Nobel check rolled in? That bounty certainly made his day, even if he did have to share it with the other winners, Israelis Shimon Peres and Yitzhak Rabin.

Anyway, some conservatives hooted at the Nobel situation and derided the President, even though he had nothing to do with the process. He was simply a beneficiary of a decision by some guys from Norway who apparently respect style over substance. I hear that eating a lot of herring leads to that.

As for the peace concept, the truth is that Barack Obama is conducting the war on terror pretty much the same way President Bush did. He's sending Predator drones into Pakistani villages to kill al-Qaeda big shots (sometimes killing civilians in the process). He's maintaining the U.S. troop presence in Iraq. He sent 30,000 more troops to Afghanistan. And, perhaps most controversial, Obama still allows the CIA to send captured terrorists to countries like Egypt, where they can get free root canals even if they don't need them.

As far as nukes are concerned, is there any sane person who wants more nuclear weapons? Just about everybody, with the possible exceptions of Kim Jong Il and the nutty Iranian mullahs, would like to get rid of the doomsday weapons. Call me cynical, but giving a speech about downsizing nukes isn't exactly a bold statement about peace. Or am I wrong?

Nevertheless, most of the world greeted Barack Obama's peace prize with rapture. French President Nicolas Sarkozy said it marked "America's return to the hearts of the world's peoples." German chancellor Angela Merkel called it an "incentive to the President and to us all to do more for world peace."

By the way, Merkel would not allow German troops to aggressively fight the terrorists in Afghanistan, thereby ensuring more violence from the Muslim killers, who are not exactly known for giving peace a chance, with apologies to John Lennon.

Ideological propaganda aside, the real reason President Obama won the Nobel Peace Prize is a Pinheaded one: he made a series of speeches, including the famous address to the Muslim world in Cairo, in which he ate humble pie on behalf of we the American people. The Norwegians *loved* that. They loved it better than North Sea oil, better than reindeer burgers.

In fact, most of the world likes Barack Obama primarily because he is the antithesis of George W. Bush. While Bush didn't give a fig what the world thought of his war on terror, Obama is apologizing for much of it, and that is a Pinheaded move. President Bush largely destroyed al-Qaeda's operational abilities, and the record shows no further foreign attacks on American soil during his watch. Mr. Obama should respect that achievement. Apparently, he does not.

My take on the Nobel Prize saga was tepid. I saw the absurdity of the decision, but unlike the hard Right, I chalked it up as a positive for America. I mean, if folks overseas like us better because they think President Obama is a peacemaker, what's the downside? In my opinion, the more people who like the USA, the better.

But some of my viewers dissented. Judy Robinson, who lives in Richmond, Indiana, wrote: "The Nobel people are a bunch of socialists. Don't give them any credence, Bill. I would be embarrassed to accept an award from them."

Shirley Venente from Kitty Hawk, North Carolina, opined: "O'Reilly, you are wrong. The award is not good for our country because it is based on a lie. Is that what we want, a lie?"

What lie, Shirley? I know for sure that the Nobel committee believes that Barack Obama is a force for peace. So no lie is involved on their part. The difficulty that some are having with the President being honored is that he had not *done* anything to earn it. But, hey, who really cares? Mr. Obama donated the money to charity, a Patriotic move, and again, having America associated with peace is not a negative, unless we back away from confronting danger. More on that coming up.

Summing up the Nobel deal: The committee people are Pinheads, committed liberals who want peace at any price. The President is blameless. Those who criticized him for being honored? Kind of petty, don't you think?

By the way, I would like to win the Nobel Peace Prize some day, so if you run into Thorby, please tell him that even though I've done nothing directly to promote world peace, I do want fewer nukes and have some Muslim friends. Should be enough.

THE GREAT RATINGS WAR

As we all know, life is a series of ups and downs, and shortly after winning the Nobel Peace Prize, President Obama entered a stunning downward cycle that damaged his administration perhaps beyond repair. There is no doubt that the autumn of 2009 was a terrible time for Barack Obama, and much of the carnage was of his own making.

The insanity began when the Obama people suddenly declared war on Fox News. By the way, shouldn't the President return the peace prize for such an aggressive action? After all, the Fox News Channel is a nonviolent enterprise with no standing army. The declaration of war from the White House came as a complete surprise to those of us who toil at FNC. You know, it was kind of like a symbolic Pearl Harbor.

But unlike America after the Japanese attack, Fox News almost immediately declared victory, because our ratings went through the roof. Folks who would never consider watching a cable news channel tuned in to see what the fight was all about. As the White House launched their verbal Predator drone missiles, my colleagues and I gleefully debated what the heck was going on.

On October 11, 2009, the Washington newspaper *The Hill* reported the opening salvo: "Fox News is simply 'a wing of the

Republican Party,' a top White House aide said today. . . . 'Fox News operates almost as either the research arm or the communications arm of the Republican Party,' [White House communications director Anita] Dunn said."

The article went on to quote some Fox News executives as saying Ms. Dunn's contention was bull and ended this way: " 'The best analogy is probably baseball,' White House press secretary Robert Gibbs told *Time* [magazine]. 'The only way to get somebody to stop crowding the plate is to throw a fastball at them. They move.' "

Or, they throw one right back at you.

Which is what FNC did.

Predictably, the left-wing media tried to come to the rescue of the Obama administration. The crazy Left *New Yorker* magazine printed this kooky analysis:

> *Half the people who watch Fox News were over sixty-three, which is the oldest demographic in the cable-news business, and, according to a poll, the majority of the ones who watch the most strident programs, such as Sean Hannity's or Bill O'Reilly's shows, were men. All that chesty fulminating apparently functions as political Cialis. Fox News shows should probably carry a warning: Contact your doctor if you have rage lasting more than four hours.*

Ho, ho, ho. Memo to the *New Yorker*: People who *declare* war are usually the ones experiencing rage, are they not?

The Pinheads at that magazine neglected to tell their readership two basic facts of the trade. First, since every news program skews older, the age differences in audience are minuscule. Second, according to a Pew Research Center study, the *Factor*'s audience is 48 percent female, a very high percentage for a news program.

Also, the *Factor* has more young (twenty-five to fifty-four) viewers than CNN, MSNBC, CNBC, and Headline News *combined*. So much for the *New Yorker* giving its readers the truth.

To be fair, the magazine did print one honest paragraph:

> *Fox News has had a robust 2009 so far, and the recent decision by the White House to declare war on the channel is not likely to put a dent in the ratings. That decision has dispirited some of the President's well-wishers [like the* New Yorker*]. It has also puzzled them.*

Indeed. It also puzzled me.

If you want to be a Patriot, you have to look at the country honestly. So let's do that vis-à-vis President Obama and Fox News. Two of my colleagues, Sean Hannity and Glenn Beck, do not like the President's policies. There is no question about that. In the morning, *Fox & Friends* guy Steve Doocy is also not a fan. But that's about it, as far as routinely hammering Mr. Obama goes. Then there is business guy Neil Cavuto, a free-market capitalist who does not accept Obama's enthusiastic spending as an effective way to juice the economy.

As for FNC's highest-rated program, *The O'Reilly Factor*: we've been very fair to the President. The folks in his administration have a standing offer to come on my program if they have a beef about anything. Anytime.

By all legitimate accounts, I conducted a probing interview of the future President in September of 2008. He said it was very fair, and it was. I've posted that interview in the last chapter of this book. Based on what has happened since, the transcript makes for interesting reading.

But back to FNC. Fox News anchorman Shepard Smith likes the President. So does Greta Van Susteren. Bret Baier is very fair to Mr. Obama, as are our political team covering the White House. No fair-minded person really disputes that.

So this charge of promoting Republican stuff is a complete myth. You may remember that John McCain did not really want to appear on the *Factor* during the campaign. And his staff actually kept Sarah Palin off the program because they feared tough questioning.

Does that sound like a GOP alliance to you?

So I do remain puzzled by the White House allegation and must enter the world of speculation for a moment to put forth an opinion on the matter. As you all know, I don't really like the theoretical world, but here goes: I believe Obama chief of staff Rahm Emanuel was the architect of the war against Fox News. The former congressman from Illinois is a left-wing ideologue who simply loathes FNC. Also, the President himself doesn't like criticism. I can identify. I don't like criticism, either, especially when it's unfair.

The problem is that reportedly the President doesn't watch much television and receives his information about cable news secondhand. From guys like Rahm Emanuel. So he's teed off at Fox News. He might not be if he actually watched us, although, to be fair, the hours from 5:00 to 6:00 P.M. and 9:00 to 10:00 P.M. would not exactly soothe Mr. Obama.

And so, there is no question that there is an animus between the Obama people and Fox News.

Quick story: After doing the aforementioned interview with then-Senator Obama in York, Pennsylvania, my staff and I had pictures taken with him. Shortly after he won the election, we sent the pictures to Obama spokesman Robert Gibbs and asked if the President would be kind enough to sign them. By the way, many of my staff voted for Obama, and mindful of the growing deficit, we included return postage.

The pictures did not come back.

So I called Gibbs and threatened to visit his house if the photos weren't returned. A few weeks later, back they came.

They were signed by autopen. We took them to Christie's auction house in New York City for verification. The writing expert we consulted actually laughed.

Thanks a lot, Robert Gibbs.

Several more weeks passed before I saw Gibbs at the White House Correspondent's dinner in Washington and gave him some grief. He said it was a terrible mistake and asked me to please resend the pictures, which I did.

Months later, President Obama wrote this note on the picture of him and me: "To Bill—I enjoyed our conversation and look forward to more in the future."

Then he signed it. Very nice, don't you think?

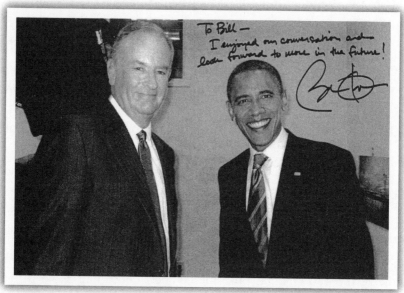

Yours truly with then-Senator Barack Obama in a photograph that took almost as many months to sign as the health care bill!

When I told my colleague Glenn Beck about the signed photo, he said I should put it alongside the one President Andrew Jackson personalized for me. Beck loves age jokes.

The whole signed picture deal is a small thing, to be sure, but it is somewhat telling and speaks to the matter of respect. I am betting big money that NBC's Brian Williams has a signed photo of him and the President hanging on his office wall, and that he did not wait more than a year to get it. Anyone care to take that wager?

Now I have a prediction: in order to demonstrate how petty I am toward the Obama administration, a number of left-wing book reviewers will pick up on the anecdote you just read and decry my "ego." They'll ignore the contextual message of the picture story and harp on my "bitterness." After writing eight books, I know these people very well. Sadly, many book reviewers are ideological Pinheads, and readers are often deceived or driven away from worthy books by their biased remarks.

But back to reality. The White House war on Fox News lasted just short of two weeks. Then other events overtook the nonsense. But it was fun while it lasted, and very profitable. Fox News increased its lead over CNN and MSNBC by even wider margins. One CNN guy told me he asked Gibbs to declare war on Larry King. I mean, why not?

Let me put one final nail in the war-on-Fox-News coffin and offer a postscript that is fascinating. By doing battle with FNC, the Obama administration attacked some Democrats and Independents as well. According to a Pew Research Center study done in 2008, the Fox News audience breaks down this way:

39 percent Republican
33 percent Democrat
22 percent Independent

So the Obama administration must not have considered the "friendly fire" factor before launching the first missile. The administration also did not count on the ultimate unintended consequence. Ready? This is really sweet.

On January 14, 2010, the Public Policy Polling organization, a company that usually works for Democrats, issued a press release with the headline: "Fox the Most Trusted Name in News?"

Here's the first part of the dispatch:

FOX THE MOST TRUSTED NAME IN NEWS?

Raleigh, N.C.—A new poll asking Americans whether they trust each of the major television news organizations in the country finds that the only one getting a positive review is Fox News. CNN does next best followed by NBC News, then CBS News, and finally ABC News.

49% of Americans say they trust Fox News to 37% who [do not]. . . . 39% say they trust [CNN] compared to 41% who do not. . . . 35% trust NBC News, 44% do not. . . .

[For CBS News the trust percentage was 32%, with 46% not trusting. ABC News clocked in at just 31% trusting, 46% not trusting.]

The release went on to say: "PPP conducted a national survey of 1,151 registered voters on January 18th and 19th. The survey's margin of error is plus or minus 2.8%."

Can you imagine the White House reaction to that poll? And it gets even worse for them. Men and women trust FNC equally. Fifty-three percent of Hispanic Americans trust Fox News, and African Americans are split: 38 percent trust us, 38 percent don't. The rest aren't sure.

The liberal media would have you believe the only people who trust FNC are angry old white guys. Apparently not. The poll says 61 percent of Americans ages eighteen to twenty-nine are confident FNC is telling them the straight story.

The Public Policy Polling exposition was a huge win for Fox

News and embarrassed the other networks, all of which have been in the news business far longer than FNC.

The culmination of all this brouhaha came during the same week, January 18–24. Stunningly, Fox News was the highest-rated cable network—not news channel—in the United States. We beat USA, ESPN, the Caterpillar Channel, everybody. Thanks again, Obama administration! And I mean that.

My hypothetical interpretation is that only one TV news network did not outwardly *root* for Barack Obama: Fox. Therefore, when things began to go south for the President, voters were reminded of that, especially after the brief "war" between us. Again, it's not that FNC is anti-Obama, it's that we are not in the proverbial tank for him, as so many other news networks and commentators are. That is why viewers are coming to us and apparently trusting us.

MAJOR GAFFE

The disastrous shoot-out with Fox News was the first in a series of events that scorched the President's cool image. On November 5, 2009, an act of terrorism rocked the country when an army psychiatrist, Major Nidal Malik Hasan, went on a rampage, murdering thirteen people and wounding twenty-nine others at Fort Hood, Texas. Almost immediately, a debate erupted over the description of the massacre: Why weren't the media and the administration calling Hasan what he obviously was, a Muslim crazy with jihad?

As each day passed, evidence that the killer was a vicious terrorist mounted. Hasan had e-mailed a top al-Qaeda recruiter in Yemen eighteen times and had a history of making jihadist statements. He also carried a business card with the letters SOA: Soldier of Allah. But some politically correct folks, mainly in the media, simply refused to describe Hasan as a Muslim terrorist, making themselves look ridiculous.

President Obama's reaction was interesting as well. Here's how the conservative *Washington Times* described it:

> *Hours after the Fort Hood massacre, a grieving nation looked to the President for consolation and leadership. Instead, it got light banter and a "shout out" before President Obama read a perfunctory statement.*
>
> *Mr. Obama was scheduled to speak at the Tribal Nations Conference hosted by the Department of the Interior's Bureau of Indian Affairs. Rather than canceling the photo op or addressing the tragedy from another venue, the President chose to open with the kind of obligatory thanks and recognition that would be appropriate in any other circumstance but not this one. The emotional shift was jarring and confusing. It was as though he were an actor switching scripts heedless of the emotional content of the event he was addressing.*
>
> *[President] Bush also suffered his critics' ire for reading* The Pet Goat *to a group of schoolchildren . . . after he was informed of the aircraft hitting the World Trade Center on September 11, 2001.*
>
> *[This] was Mr. Obama's* Pet Goat *moment.*

Only it wasn't.

The national media quickly buried the story, leaving it to the conservative ideologues on talk radio. Although a few liberal organizations like the *Boston Globe* did criticize the President's initial remarks, the media largely protected him.

So was the Fort Hood gaffe really that big a deal? The answer is no. Mr. Obama made a mistake, as Presidents often do. He also urged the nation to avoid "jumping to conclusions" about Major Hasan—nothing wrong with a call for temperance when emotions are running high. No, the President's reactions to the Fort Hood horror were not a big deal. But his failure to confront the evil involved in the massacre is.

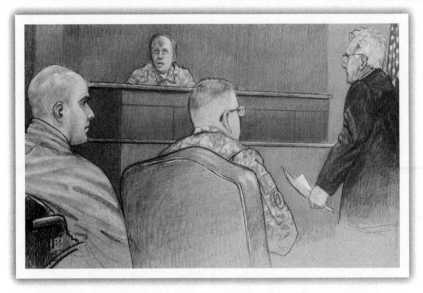

Major Nidal Hasan (*left*), the psychiatrist accused of gunning down thirteen people in Fort Hood, Texas, appears at a pretrial hearing.

The pattern we are seeing with President Obama is that evil doesn't really matter all that much; it's treated as just another bump in the road. We now know that Hasan was a troubled man who got preferential treatment, despite prior instances of disturbing behavior and poor performance reviews, because he's a Muslim. That insane situation directly led to the deaths of thirteen people.

Did President Obama address that situation? No, he did not. That is not the President's style. Unlike President Bush the Younger and Ronald Reagan before him, Mr. Obama does not like to confront people with their sins. There is no "Axis of Evil" or "Evil Empire" rhetoric coming out of the Obama White House. That would be too "divisive." Instead, the President prides himself on keeping cool while dealing with destructive elements. No heated dress-downs for him . . . unless we're talking about Fox News personnel.

The problem with that approach is that it goes against the American way. We are a nation that makes value judgments and demands that the bad guys pay a price. Hasan is a terrorist, and that's that. Most Americans reject nuance when dealing with mass murderers, and they don't give a fig about political correctness.

Writing in the *Wall Street Journal*, former CIA officer Reuel Marc Gerecht was blunt about Mr. Obama's lack of passion in the face of persistent terrorism:

> *President Barack Obama's determined effort not to mention Islam in terrorist discussions—which means that we must not suggest Major Hasan's murderous activities flowed from his faith—will weaken American counterterrorism. Worse, the President's position is an enormous wasted opportunity to advance an all-critical Muslim debate about the nature and legitimacy of jihad.*
>
> *[Obama] could ask, as some Muslims have, why is it that Islam has produced so many jihadists? Why is it that Major Hasan's rampage has produced so little questioning among Muslim clerics about why a man, one in a long line of Muslim militants, so easily takes God's name to slaughter his fellow citizens?*

TRIAL AND ERROR

That analysis leads us to the discussion of one of the most absurd decisions I have ever seen a President make: civilian trials for 9/11 mastermind Khalid Sheikh Mohammed and four of his al-Qaeda thug friends.

As you most likely know, on November 13, 2009, Attorney General Eric Holder announced that KSM would be tried in a New York City federal court and that the government would seek the death penalty. Holder acknowledged that the terrorist could have been placed in front of a military tribunal, which would have protected national security information far better than the civilian system will. Military trials are also much less expensive.

By the way, when Holder made his controversial announcement President Obama was in Asia. Far away. Not close by.

Khalid Sheikh Mohammed is a hard-core al-Qaeda operative who admitted planning the attacks on the World Trade Center and Washington, D.C. He also says he personally beheaded *Wall Street Journal* reporter Daniel Pearl.

After his capture in Pakistan, KSM was waterboarded and held at Guantánamo Bay for more than three years, so some believe that the Obama administration wanted to allow a full exposition of KSM's captivity in order to embarrass the Bush administration. That's speculation, but the initial decision to try the terrorists in New York City makes little sense unless there was indeed some kind of political component.

Anger mounted as reports said the trial was estimated to take years and could cost as much as $800 million, a tab that the taxpayers would have to pick up. Lawyers for the terrorists said openly that they intended to put the United States on trial. It is a foregone conclusion that the thugs are guilty, so the only thing they have to gain is the opportunity to spread al-Qaeda propaganda, which the terrorists would almost certainly do. Just look at how Faisal Shahzad, the Pakistani-born terrorist who admitted trying to set off a bomb in Times Square, used his arraignment hearing as a press op for his anti-American "cause."

They love this stuff in Islamabad.

The word *Pinhead* does not even come close to describing what kind of person would support giving these killers more of a worldwide propaganda forum. I am on record as admiring Barack Obama's intelligence and drive. But the New York City/KSM deal was flat-out stupid, and every poll showed that most Americans realized that. For example, a Gallup poll taken a few days after the KSM announcement showed 59 percent of Americans favoring military justice for old Khalid and his mates. Just 36 percent supported the ridiculous civilian venue.

Rep. Steve King (R-IA) addresses the impact of bringing Khalid Sheikh Mohammed and other terror suspects to American soil for trial.

In addition, the Obama administration's desire to allow these killers another shot at demeaning America brought pain to the families and friends of those murdered on 9/11. In my area on Long Island, hundreds of innocent people woke up that terrible morning, went to work, and never came back. And the President turns around and tells surviving family members that al-Qaeda members captured overseas are entitled to U.S. constitutional protections? What a foolish, foolish decision. And one that hurt the President's job approval rating. It was just a matter of time before that confounding decision had to be reversed. Unfortunately, the President took his time righting this wrong, the same way he took his time deploying additional troops to Afghanistan. In the interim, the chaos made him look weak.

Remember, Mr. Obama told CNN that he did not personally order the decision to try KSM and the others in New York City but had allowed Holder to make it "based on the law." The President also said KSM and his pals would be found guilty and executed.

Upon hearing that, ACLU lawyers jotted down these words: "polluted jury."

A few days later, in a bizarre display in front of the Senate Judiciary Committee, Attorney General Holder seemed befuddled by questions about his decision. He dodged and weaved before Senator Lindsey Graham of South Carolina finally knocked him out.

Lindsey Graham: Can you give me one case in United States history where an enemy combatant caught on the battlefield was tried in civilian court?

Eric Holder: I don't know, I'd have to look at that, you know, the determination.

Lindsey Graham: We're making history here, Mr. Attorney General. I'll answer it for you, and the answer is: None.

By the middle of November 2009 Barack Obama's job approval rating was crashing. The softness he showed on Fort Hood and the mind-boggling Khalid Sheikh Mohammed decision had made a deep impression. Also, the continuing health care chaos weighed heavily on his image, as did his reluctance to make a decision about sending more troops to Afghanistan. On November 18 the Rasmussen daily tracking poll of likely voters had showed 52 percent of Americans disapproving of the President's job performance. That is a stunning number for a President who took office just ten months earlier with approval numbers in the high 60s because of his pledge to bring change we can believe in.

Roughly four months later, the Obama administration put up a white flag. During the first week in March 2010 unnamed "White House sources" whispered to Fox News and the *Washington Post* that the President was "rethinking" Holder's plan to try KSM in New York and most likely would return him and four other al-Qaeda thugs to the military for trial.

You can imagine how *that* went over in San Francisco, where the liberal ideology reigns.

Actually, for those clear-thinking Americans who want a robust defense against fanatical al-Qaeda members, the Khalid fiasco turned out to be a positive. Because the President had no idea what to do with the man and his cohorts, the prison at Guantánamo Bay remained open far longer than many Obama supporters thought it would. As time marched on, Khalid and his gang continued to cool their heels behind the barbed-wire-ringed facility. Attorney General Holder tried his hardest to give the al-Qaeda members a forum but failed dismally. Have I called Holder a Pinhead yet?

FIRE AND ICE

The presidential election of 2008 is just a distant memory for many of us, but one thing is clear: eighteen months after President Obama's triumphant inauguration, the country had turned on him. A Gallup poll on June 24, 2010, said that 62 percent of Americans believed the country was heading in the wrong direction. That was the highest number since before Mr. Obama won the election. So what went wrong?

Did the Pinhead factor just kick in? What is the story behind the story? The answer to that question may lie in a committed left-wing ideology or perhaps in hubris, but most likely it is to be found in a different personality trait. President Obama is a loner, a man who lives deep within himself. While many of us feel the pain of others around us, the President is more of a technician, a man slow to respond outwardly to any emotion. It would not be fair to say he doesn't identify with others, but his public persona is definitely detached.

My analysis explains why the President could be great friends with the Reverend Jeremiah Wright, the America-hater. Obama's interaction with Wright was all about Obama. Period. Not about the country. The thinking, hypothetically, goes like this: So what if Wright spouted anti-American stuff? Who really cares? He offered spiritual guidance, and the President honored that with a form of friendship. What Wright did or said apart from Obama did not seem to matter to the politician.

In the same way, the President's personality may explain his take on the subject of Muslim terrorism. The President views it as a major problem to be solved, not an evil to be eradicated. While President Bush took 9/11 personally—as an outrage that must be avenged—President Obama sees it as a catastrophe that must not be allowed to happen again.

It is all about emotion. Americans are largely an emotional people. We feel things deeply. But the President is able to rise above emotion, a skill that has served him well up to now. He survived a childhood that would have emotionally crippled many other children. And he later overcame the powerful Clinton machine to win the presidency. In more than one instance, his cool has won the fight.

But in running the country, the President often appears to be separating himself from the common folks. Many can't believe that he is not feeling and identifying with their anger and pain. It seems that he is not, as they say in California, "in the moment" with their concerns. Those who pay close attention to Mr. Obama's actions and words are picking up a kind of coldness. Wrong-headed decisions combined with a lack of passion when dealing with evil could wind up derailing the Obama vision. If, in fact, there actually *is* a vision.

The oil spill disaster only highlighted the passion problem. As millions of people began suffering from the massive pollution, Mr. Obama remained kind of detached. It took him nearly two months to actually address the problem from the Oval Office, and then when he did, the speech was flat. Even his supporters on MSNBC and CNN laced into him. Why didn't he do something right away? Why was he not showing more fire?

The answers: (1) He didn't know what to do, and (2) fire is not his style of governance. Ice is.

Let me repeat: I don't find him personally cold or unfeeling, as you will see in just a moment. But, for whatever reasons or lessons learned in a lifetime, this man, reportedly a skilled poker player, keeps things close to his chest. Will he change, or will we come to accept his style? One or the other has to happen or he'll begin working on his memoirs in 2012.

A WARMER CLIMATE

As the year 2009 wound down, I met up with President Obama once again. On December 15 I attended the White House Christmas party for broadcast Pinheads. Actually, I was kind of surprised to be invited. Only a few of the dreaded Fox News crew were. Brit Hume, Bret Baier, Greta Van Susteren, and I each received nifty engraved invitations, and we lined up on a brisk night on Pennsylvania Avenue. After a few minutes, the Secret Service along with White House staffers checked IDs and we entered the White House, which, for me, is always a thrill. I brought along my ten-year-old daughter, Madeline, who tried to feign boredom, but I could see her eyes widening.

I must say the party was "smashing," to use a term I picked up while living in London. And when my daughter and I were brought in to greet the President and First Lady, they could not have been nicer.

I was very impressed with Michelle Obama, who commands the room with her physical presence and was as welcoming as a person could be. She discussed the pop singer Taylor Swift with Madeline while I gave the President some jazz about his boast that he could beat me one-on-one in basketball by spotting me ten points in an eleven-point game. (That dialogue happened during my interview with him on the campaign trail. See page 236.)

I reminded the President that I was ready to take that bet. He said that I looked to be in better shape than the last time we met. I answered, "That's because you're keeping me on my toes, sir."

Two alpha males circling. I could almost envision Michelle Obama rolling her eyes. I'm sure Madeline was.

I appreciated the warmth and kindness the Obamas showed my daughter. They did not have to go out of their way like that. For them, the party was an exhausting three-hour marathon of greetings and good tidings. It takes discipline and grace to do that well. Perhaps a small thing in the big scheme of life, but the President and First Lady were Patriots on that night.

After I reported on the evening to the *Factor* audience, I received a few nasty e-mails from the Obama-haters, but not that many. Laura Ingraham gave me some static, but I gave it right back to her. As I said earlier, there is no reason to disrespect the President of the United States. Disagree, fine. But a certain Patriotic respect should be shown. The man is not *always* wrong.

Still, three days after the party, I had to make fun of the President on the air because of the climate conference he attended in Copenhagen. I mean, come on. That incredible dog-and-pony show cost American taxpayers millions of dollars, and what was accomplished? Some countries said, "Yeah, pollution is bad and we're going to clean up our acts. Only don't give us mandates or deadlines, and by the way, we won't allow any verification of our environmental efforts. Other than that, we are down with combating warming! Please pass the lingonberry sauce."

President Obama lent his authority to the conference, which is not in itself a bad thing. If people pay more attention to cleaning up the world, that is a positive, whether you believe in global warming or not. But Mr. Obama tried to spin the conference as some kind of break-through deal, which it certainly was not. That sleight of verbal hand offended fans of no spin. Little of substance was achieved in Copenha-gen. Even the anarchists rioting in the streets did not liven things up.

MERRY CHRISTMAS, MR. PRESIDENT

With all that had occurred by the end of 2009, Barack Obama had to be happy he was set to enjoy Christmas in Hawaii, his birth state. With visions of sugarplums and Diamond Head dancing in his head, he flew west with his family to the beautiful islands. But the happy holiday didn't last long.

On Christmas Day, a crazy young jihadist named Umar Abdul-mutallab tried to blow up a Northwest jetliner flying from Amster-dam to Detroit, Michigan. Umar, whose own father had warned the American embassy in Lagos that his son was hanging with al-Qaeda, somehow boarded the plane with explosives in his underpants. When he tried to ignite them, they fizzled and some passengers jumped him. The plane then landed safely, thanks to those brave civilians.

As you'll remember, the story was enormous. Despite billions spent on national security, a twenty-three-year-old loon trained in Yemen almost murdered three hundred people on a plane. It took President Obama three days to respond publicly, and when he did, he called the terrorist guy an "isolated extremist."

Not good enough.

The Right went nuts, and the President was hammered, even though it had taken President Bush six days to comment on Richard

Reid, the shoe bomber, back in 2002. At that time, the U.S. antiterror security program was just beginning. That's not an excuse for Mr. Bush, it's just a note of interest. But today Americans expect their government to aggressively protect them against al-Qaeda and other killers. This incident embarrassed the entire American intelligence community, and Mr. Obama's dispassionate response only added to the hysteria.

Finally, under withering pressure, President Obama gave a speech in which he said that the country was at war with al-Qaeda and he would correct the mistakes made. The President looked grave and sounded, for once, severely teed off. But even liberals expressed doubts about the depth of his grasp of the issue.

Writing in the *New York Times,* we again turn to lefty columnist Maureen Dowd who put it this way:

> *When [Obama] failed to immediately step up to the microphones in Hawaii after the Christmas terrors and thank the passengers for bravely foiling the plot that his intelligence community had failed to see, President Cool reached the limits of cool.*
>
> *No Drama Obama is reticent about displays of emotion. The Spock in him needs to exert mental and emotional control. This is why he stubbornly insists on staying aloof and setting his own deliberate pace for responding—whether it's in a debate or after a debacle. But it's not okay to be cool about national security when Americans are scared.*

Ms. Dowd must be a *Factor* watcher, because that was the same drum I was beating. To effectively lead the nation in times of crisis, you have to feel what the folks are feeling. As stated, cool may have won the election, but cool is losing the public's support on the terror front. How about some *anger* here? Some terrorist tries to wipe out hundreds of civilians on Christmas Day, but our leader doesn't condemn the action immediately? Come on. If you can't get worked up about a mass murder attempt and the gross incompetence of those responsible for protecting Americans, what can you get worked up about?

This body scanner at a security checkpoint in Schiphol Airport in the Netherlands might have detected the device used in the Christmas Day attempt to blow up a Detroit-bound airliner, if U.S. authorities hadn't told Amsterdam's airport not to use it on United States–bound flights due to privacy concerns.

No Drama Obama. That image won't work in the long run. The President has to step up his urgency level if he wants to be two-termer Obama.

Unfortunately, the President had pretty much the same distanced demeanor a few months later when authorities arrested another jihadist nut for trying to blow up Times Square in New York City. Now, I'm not suggesting Mr. Obama go all Lewis Black on us when he speaks about attempted terror attacks, but understating an attempted mass homicide is something only a Pinhead would do. Is it not?

FOURTH-QUARTER GRADES

With so much in play at the end of 2009, let's give President Obama a P&P report card for the last quarter of that chaotic year:

Fort Hood.

The President was only a minor Pinhead for not forcefully speaking out against violent fanaticism.

The Christmas Day terror attack.

He was a big Pinhead this time for not reacting in a way that folks could identify with. To repeat, Americans are furious that Islamic terrorism continues to threaten the country. The President should reflect on that fact and perhaps change his subdued tone.

Al-Qaeda civilian trials.

No question about it—POTUS was a major Pinhead for allowing this atrocity to take place. Nothing good will come of it, just wait and see. When the underwear guy was taken off the plane on Christmas and sent to a federal prison to see his lawyer, you could hear the gnashing of teeth all the way to Waikiki. Such coddling of terrorists could very well be the undoing of Barack Obama.

Afghanistan.

The commander in chief definitely qualifies as a Patriot for finally giving his field commanders the resources they need to fight the Taliban. Although it was annoying that the decision took so long to be implemented, I understand the complexity of the theater. When I visited Afghanistan in 2007, I was amazed at how primitive the place is. Did you know that life expectancy in Afghanistan is just north of forty years? That ranks among the worst in the world.

Global warming.

On this issue President Cool gets a mixed grade. He is a Patriot for wanting a cleaner planet, but a Pinhead for buying into theoretical nonsense. Worldwide pollution is a dangerous situation that deserves a serious hearing. Al Gore's scare tactics are not the solution; finding common ground is. Everybody should agree that less pollution is good. Let's start there and leave the ideological component home.

Energy level.

On this final point our tireless leader is a Patriot. President Obama works extremely hard.

Summing up, 2009 began with great expectations and ended with a country divided and exhausted by a brutal economy, ideological divides, and implacable enemies abroad. The young President got quite a dose of reality throughout his first year in office, and as we know, how a person handles adversity will eventually define his or her ultimate Pinhead or Patriot status.

CHAPTER 3

To Your Health

IF BARACK OBAMA THOUGHT the last few months of 2009 were rough, well, the opening weeks of 2010 made them look like a piece of chocolate layer cake. Ladies and gentlemen, let the Tea Parties begin!

Exasperated by record-breaking government spending and a confusing health care bill that the President could not explain, thousands of everyday Americans began publicly demonstrating against the perceived signs of "socialism" and, in general, the liberal tendencies of the Obama administration.

Led by Fox News commentator and radio talk show host Glenn Beck, and featuring high-profile encouragement from Sarah Palin, the so-called Tea Party movement blasted into the national consciousness.

But it was largely the ugly attacks against this group that drew them further into the spotlight and kept them there for so long.

Here's what I mean. Some committed left-wing commentators on NBC and CNN quickly branded the protestors as "teabaggers," a crude sexual slang term that is associated with oral sex. Because of their divisive tactics, these media Pinheads not only brought huge attention to the Tea Party movement, but their vitriol also angered many nonpartisan Americans, making the Tea Party message more readily acceptable.

My take on the Tea Party movement is simple and, I think, Patriotic. These folks are practicing the time-honored tradition of public dissent. They are brave enough to make their political feelings public, which, I believe, shows love of country.

Tea Party protesters steep in the heat of a tax revolt rally in Washington, D.C.

As we all know, the Tea Party attackers in the media did not demean the Iraq antiwar movement, did they? Certainly not. So liberal media people, let me get this straight: if you sympathize with a protest, it's legitimate, but if you disagree with the message, it's not. That doesn't sound very American to me. How does it sound to you?

The same thing was true of the Minuteman movement, which

protested illegal immigration across the Mexican border. These men and women were immediately branded as "racist" by some in the liberal media because they wanted an end to the immigration chaos. Doesn't it strike you as strange that the liberal movement in the United States is so intolerant? I mean, isn't the left-wing mantra "individual freedom"? Have liberals stopped believing that America is a place where diversity of thought is encouraged? I always thought the liberal handbook promoted political activism. "Power to the people," right? Sure. Today that handbook would more accurately read, "Power to the people who agree with us; obscene names to those who don't." Some of you may remember the term *hippie fascism* that floated around during the late 1960s. Everything was mellow, man, until you questioned the movement. Then it wasn't far out anymore. It was, what the F is wrong with you?

Thinking back, I was surprised that CNN correspondent Anderson Cooper joined the Far Left chorus regarding the Tea Party folks. Cooper is a solid reporter who, despite sympathizing with the Left on many things, has forged a respectable career out of being fair. To be equally fair to him, Cooper did apologize for his use of the term *teabagger*, but in the eyes of some reasonable folks, his initial comments demeaned him. On that occasion, Anderson Cooper was a Pinhead.

It isn't even worth commenting on the vile stuff coming from NBC's cable news arm. Suffice it to say that it is Pinhead Central over there.

CLEAN BILL OF HEALTH?

As the first few months of 2010 unfolded, the health care debate exploded into a national battle. President Obama found himself defending a huge new entitlement that would, among other things, force Americans to buy health insurance or possibly suffer financial penalties. The President urged us to support his vision of providing

58 ✳ Bill O'Reilly

more than 30 million uninsured citizens with a chance to improve their lives. What the President did not emphasize, however, was that 60 percent of the newly insured would have to be subsidized by you and me, the American taxpayers.

Vice President Joe Biden is overheard telling President Obama, "This is a big f——— deal," after introducing the President at the health care bill-signing ceremony on March 23, 2010.

The President also claimed that ObamaCare would actually reduce America's deficit by bringing down health care costs, a vital component of the overall plan, as the USA currently owes about $14 trillion to its creditors and could very well slip into bankruptcy down the road. Despite Mr. Obama's passion, every Republican in Congress disputed the President's financial numbers, and, polls showed, so did most Americans.

Nevertheless, on Sunday, March 20, ObamaCare passed the House, and two days later the President signed it into law. The highlight of the subsequent victory lap was Vice President Joe Biden telling Mr. Obama in front of a microphone that the situation was a "big f—— deal." No argument with that, and don't you just love Biden in front of a mic? I mean, the man becomes absolutely possessed!

But winning the ObamaCare battle is not a full victory. The President has to hope he hasn't lost the war. There is no question that the new law will do some good and may improve some lives, but it is still at the expense of other tax-paying Americans. It is also a fact that to get national health care passed, Barack Obama badly damaged his well-honed image as a new-style politician. The Democratic Party is now associated with Western European–style top-down governance. In traditional America, that is a precarious place to be.

DEAL OR NO DEAL

For the record, and as part of our Pinhead-or-Patriot assessment, let's take a look at the "back-room deal" factor. In order to get support for his controversial bill, the President had to okay the following:

- a special deal that exempts 800,000 Floridians from any Medicare Advantage cuts;
- a $300 million increase in spending for the state of Louisiana alone;
- a $100 million guarantee for hospital construction in Connecticut;
- a $2 billion increase in Medicare spending for Nevada, Wyoming, Montana, and Utah;
- a $600 million Medicare spending boost for Vermont, plus almost the same amount for Massachusetts (a state that already has universal health care requirements); and
- an extra $850 billion in Medicaid funds for Arizona, Delaware, Hawaii, Maine, Massachusetts (again),

Minnesota, New York, Pennsylvania, Vermont (again), Washington, Wisconsin, and the District of Columbia.

That's just a partial list of the deals struck behind the scenes to ensure passage of ObamaCare. Remember, the President campaigned on "change we can believe in." But these quid pro quo deals have been around since the Continental Congress. Call me a Pinhead, but I'm not seeing much *change* in the legislative process. If ObamaCare is really so good, the folks would have lined up behind it.

They did not.

And here's the kicker. The President says that the massive Obama-Care expense, estimated to reach close to $1 trillion, will be paid for largely by cuts in Medicare spending. But not only is there speculation that costs will come in way higher than that, check out the chart on the previous page of special deals again, and you will clearly see significant *increases* in Medicare spending. The whole deal is a recipe for cynicism pie.

There is no question that the President and most Democrats believe that the ends justify the means in health care reform. On the other side, the conservative opposition is pulling out all the anti-Obama stops. In fact, even I, your humble correspondent, got hammered in that wordstorm. . . .

RUSHING TO CONCLUSIONS

Perhaps the most vociferous anti-Obama guy in the country is radio commentator Rush Limbaugh. To say that Mr. Limbaugh and the President see things differently is like saying Michael Moore needs a personal trainer. There is no doubt.

A few weeks before ObamaCare passed the House, we had a series of debates on the *Factor* about whether or not the President is a closet socialist. I said he was not because he wasn't actively trying to control private property, which is what socialists do. I did say, however, that Mr. Obama believes in some socialist tenets, such as income redistribution and the imposition of social justice through legislation or even through the use of executive orders. By the way, I said that to the President's face during my interview with him, which you can read at the end of this book.

Anyway, Rush Limbaugh took exception to my analysis of President Obama's belief system and brought my name up while talking to a caller on his radio show. Here's what he had to say (with some of my thoughts interjected throughout in the gray-shaded boxes):

Rush Limbaugh: Let's pretend that you're talking to Bill O'Reilly.

Caller: Okay.

Rush: What do you think of me? Where have I gone wrong today?

Caller: You're asking me what I think of Bill O'Reilly?

Rush: No, I am Bill O'Reilly. What do you think of me? Tell me where I've gone wrong today.

Caller: He does say that a lot.

> At this point, El Rushbo has set me up as a target of derision. He didn't say to his listeners flat out, "Hey, I'm going to mock O'Reilly." Instead he is pretending to be me in a satiric riff. He continues.

Rush: Look, all I'm telling you is that you've gotta give socialism a fair shake for the folks. I'm not gonna sit here and condemn it like these right-wingers are. We've got to give socialism a fair shake, and we here at the *Factor* are going to give socialism, even communism, a fair shake. We'll do an in-depth investigation and we'll report back because we're not knee-jerking and we are looking out for the folks . . . we just don't like all this Obama-bashing here at the *Factor*, that's for these extreme right-wingers. This Obama-bashing is not productive, the Bush-bashing wasn't productive. We're going to give socialism and the destruction of the country a fair examination, and if we determine that Obama's destroying the country, we'll report it fairly.

> That is the heart of Limbaugh's annoyance, that I have criticized some conservatives for overdoing the socialistic stuff. Apparently, Rush does not agree with me.

Caller: Bill O'Reilly, sir, I think Obama is the most arrogant, egotistical man I have ever known.

Rush: I don't care about that. What do you think of me? Am I arrogant, too? If Obama's arrogant, nobody can be more arrogant than I am. What do you think of me, where have I gone wrong here?

> The "arrogant" charge is interesting. I'm not confirming or denying my arrogance or anyone else's. I will say this, however. If you state an opinion with authority in this country, you will be branded as arrogant, that's just the way we are. I believe Rush Limbaugh may have experienced that himself. Or am I wrong, Rush?

So here's the question: Was Limbaugh being a Pinhead during that routine? Or does he have me down pat? You make the call.

I've met Rush Limbaugh a couple of times, but we've never had an actual conversation. Whenever the left-wing press attacks me, saying that I am some kind of conservative zealot, I smile and think of old Rush. He would certainly disagree.

Mr. Limbaugh analyzes current events from a conservative perspective and is totally up-front about it. So are Sean Hannity and most other right-wing commentators. They tell you exactly who they are, and from there the game is on. If you are on the Left, you'll get mocked for sure. If you are someone like me, a traditional-minded independent, you will not be trusted. It's all about orthodoxy. The rules of radio talk are rigid and time-honored. Speaking to the choir can be extremely profitable, and there's nothing wrong with doing that. The choir needs entertainment, too!

By contrast, my analysis of Barack Obama and everything else in the public arena is fact-based, not ideological. The President, as I've suggested, cannot be accurately branded a "socialist" until he starts messing around with private property. You can rightly call some of his policies "socialistic"—and I have—but saying Obama is the El Norte version of Hugo Chávez is absurd.

Still, I kind of enjoyed being called "arrogant" by Rush Limbaugh. Not too many folks reach that plateau in life. My eighth-grade teacher agreed with Rush, so maybe he's on to something. And here's an interesting point. There is an important difference between being attacked by a guy like Limbaugh on the Right and, say, the Media Matters outfit on the Left: Limbaugh seeks to *mock* me, while the Matters fanatics want to *harm* me. The intent of the scrutiny is very interesting. It is sticks and stones versus take him out. So I react accordingly.

★

CHAPTER 4

Your Place in a Changing America

THE FIRST DECADE of the twenty-first century was brutal for many of us. The terror attack on 9/11 dramatically changed the country, and then the vicious recession that began in the fall of 2008 altered it yet again. The working American was assaulted by attacks from Muslim jihadists overseas, then suffered because greedy corporate investors right here at home ransacked America's financial system. Both of these assaults damaged our security in very personal ways.

Unfortunately, meaningful security requires money (although the harsh truth is that you can never be fully protected). Since your humble correspondent has been both poor and rich in his life (and has been the man in the middle along the way, too), I've learned firsthand how difficult all positions can be. But let's focus on the two extremes first.

RICH MAN, POOR MAN

The impoverished person is simply worn down by how few options are available to him or her, while the wealthy person is worn down by having to be on guard *all the time*. If you have money, chances are someone else wants to take it from you. The more assets you have, the more security you need. The fewer assets you have, the less security you're able to buy. Poor people are at the mercy of many things they cannot control. Rich people are at the mercy of bad people who target them.

Perhaps the ultimate Pinhead in the world of wealth is the swindler Bernie Madoff, whose Ponzi scheme caused at least $65 billion to go up in flames and many people to get burned in the process. Here's a guy who betrayed his family, friends, and business associates without remorse. If you examine the Madoff file, you will see an example of true evil. Some folks I know can't understand evil; they don't even think it exists.

Swindler Bernie Madoff, who faced a prison sentence of up to 150 years, arrives at federal court in New York, where he pleaded guilty to charges that he engineered one of the largest investment scams in U.S. history.

But exist it does, and Madoff is one of the dark side's most devious poster boys. He fleeced wealthy clients and friends, completely ruining many of them. One day they were in control of their lives; the next day whatever financial security they thought they had was completely gone. *And nobody could bring it back.*

Think about that for a moment. You work hard all your life to provide stability and prosperity for yourself and your loved ones, then a country club criminal, a lowlife punk in a three-thousand-dollar suit, steals it. And there is absolutely nothing you can do. Nothing.

The message here is that evil chases all of us. Most of the time it comes in small doses, not supersize Madoff-type doses, so the world around us doesn't always notice as much. Right now, some Americans feel that the federal government is evil, too, and that society, in general, is going to hell. So let's take a look at both of those points of view.

TO HELL IN A HANDBASKET?

There is no question that American society is changing. Polls show that atheism is on the rise and organized religion is in decline. On the secular front, we've seen the legalization of soft drugs and of gay marriage in some places, and because many teachers are committed liberals, our children are being educated in a system that skews left big-time. Do such things bode well for us?

As I've written in previous books, I have always believed there is great strength in the Judeo-Christian tradition, and while I know that I am a sinner, I try my best to embrace principles like self-reliance, loyalty, and fairness. I also do not judge the personal conduct of others, leaving that to a deity whom I believe not only exists but is active in the world.

Evaluating public policy, not private behavior, is my primary job, although if the two converge in a way that's harmful to you, then I could be vocal about it, as I will be below on the subject of celebrity scandals invading our lives. And if I'm truly and deeply concerned about it, I could swing into action, as I have over the vicious attack the Westboro Baptist Church launched on Lance Corporal Matthew Snyder's family, which warrants its own discussion in chapter 6.

Let's begin with the example of Tiger Woods. This is a case where a celebrity's indiscretions didn't necessarily hurt the public—they simply provided titillation. But it was actually the mass marketing of the scandal that I believe hurt everyone—not just Tiger, his wife, and the sport of golf, but you and me and even the kids who were exposed to the all-pervasive coverage.

The embarrassing exposition had to be reported as a matter of public record, but the *Factor* stayed away from reveling in the man's misery, primarily because only Pinheads enjoy watching others experience pain.

Is Woods a Pinhead? In the scandal area, certainly. He hurt his family and others who admired him. And if you enjoyed that story, you are a Pinhead as well. It is simply not noble to derive satisfaction from the suffering of others, even if they deserve it. I did not feel the golfer's pain, but I did empathize with the collapse of a fellow human being and the suffering of those around him. Like his wife. Like his mother. I did not enjoy reading about that case, especially when accusers and their lawyers greedily scurried out from under their rocks.

So it is true that all of us Americans are experiencing cultural changes on many different levels. Some are legislated, some are not. Some of these changes are compounded and even magnified by repeated images in the media. This kind of attention not only turns private hurt into public shame but also runs the risk of desensitizing us as a culture, too.

But let's shift the focus now from the superstar to the average Joe.

THE MAN IN THE MIDDLE

The individual American appears to be rapidly losing power. Wages have been pretty much stagnant for more than a decade. Working people are getting by but not moving up. It is damned difficult to pay your bills and taxes and also save a few bucks, is it not?

President Obama and his team want to pass laws that put even more power and money in the hands of the federal government; that, very simply, is my primary beef with them. The more shots are called from Washington, the fewer options we the people have in our own lives. Rugged individualism made this country great, not entitlement programs rigged to provide "income redistribution."

The health care mess is a perfect example of what I'm talking about. The problems in the health system might have been solved without a massive government intrusion in the following ways: a combination of strict federal oversight on insurance, drug, and medical concerns along with increased health insurance competition across state lines, as well as tort reform so that corrupt lawyers cannot bankrupt medical people. All of these together would have brought health care costs down significantly. We'll provide more details on this later.

But a marketplace solution is not what progressive Americans really want. Misleading political rhetoric aside, their vision is for the feds to control health care and pretty much every other industry. In that way, Washington could impose the big liberal tenet of "economic justice" on the country. I delve deeply into this strategy in my book *Culture Warrior*. Briefly put, for the committed Left, an economy controlled by the government combined with punitive taxation of the rich is "change you can believe in." In the 2008 presidential campaign, John McCain failed to make voters understand what Barack Obama really had in mind. Senator McCain simply did not spell out the freedom issue: Do you want to control your life, or do you want the Obama administration to do it for you?

That's why the Tea Party people are so angry. They don't want the government running their lives and spending so much money that the United States becomes insolvent. But the freedom message that many Tea Party protesters promote is being lost because a dishonest national press is portraying the movement as fringe Far Right hysteria. This is another huge change in America: a partisan press using its power to demonize those who do not adhere to a left-wing view of life. Once the Tea Party folks showed up wearing sweatshirts and baseball caps, they became targets for the elite snobs who dominate the mainstream media. Yes, most of them are Pinheads; they just can't help it. If an everyday American is in view, many media people feel the need to sigh. Don't you just love that?

SOME HONEY WITH THAT TEA?

Unfortunately, some Tea Party people play into the bogus Far Right stereotype by demonizing President Obama in crude ways. If instead they were to concentrate on freedom and avoid personal attacks, they might prosper more in the future. Most Americans respond to the freedom issue and do not yet realize that their own options in life are being substantially eroded in the age of Obama.

That being said, I don't despise President Obama because he's a big-government liberal. I just think his philosophy will weaken the country in both the long and short run. I could be wrong, and the President could be right. We'll see. As I have said before, I admire what the President has accomplished in his life (please don't tell Rush Limbaugh) and how he overcame a childhood that could have ruined him. There is much good in Mr. Obama's story, but his overall philosophy remains questionable, as many Americans are beginning to understand.

By the way, on the *Factor*, I have urged the President to hire me as his top adviser. If he would do that one thing, all would turn out okay. My first move would be to bring some Tea Party people to the White House. I wouldn't serve up a pot of Earl Grey, but maybe some beer and soda. Kinda like that Massachusetts cop and professor deal. Détente is good. It's Patriotic.

THE TECH OFFENSIVE

Let's leave politics for a moment and examine a huge danger that is looming large in America: the rise of the machines! I'm not playing around. High-tech gizmos are now dominating the lives of many Americans, particularly the young. With so much time being spent in unreal digital precincts, interpersonal relationships, beginning with family life, are suffering. This dramatic change is already affecting us all, and it will only get worse as the machines become even more sophisticated and, for some, addictive.

Here's a good example. No longer are loyalty and true friendship admired or even sought after in many quarters. What's being sold today in their place is instant gratification. Just turn on a computer, and you can create your own world. Who needs to deal with real problems and come up with effective solutions when escape is only a finger-click away? Why bother cultivating close personal relationships when you can chat with thousands and never even leave your home?

I see the machine culture thriving among some of the younger people working at Fox News. Their entire lives revolve around gadgets: iPods, cell phones, BlackBerries, what have you. Their attention is usurped and their minds are constantly cluttered by these toys. When I encourage big-picture thinking and creative storytelling, I get a lot of blank stares. With machines constantly pulsating signals inside their heads, it is hard for young people to develop insights and problem-solving skills. Will the USA become a nation of robots? Could happen.

Don't get me wrong, I see how these gadgets have worked to some people's short-term advantage, but it's the long term I'm interested in. It was the high-tech age that made it so much easier for Barack Obama's nonspecific message of hope and change to catch fire. In fact, his use of flashy gizmos also contributed to the perception that John McCain was old-fashioned. Obama represented the quick-text-message era, while McCain seemed to harken back to the old rotary phone (if you know what that is).

Just the same, John McCain is a true Patriot. I selected him as my 2009 "Person of the Year" because he consistently stood up for what is right during a very turbulent year.

You may remember that it was Senator McCain who told the world that the Iranian dissidents who are trying to overthrow that awful government needed international support. He urged apathetic nations to rally around freedom-loving Iranians, but few countries did—not even the United States. President Obama's posture indicated that America was not going to intrude in Iran's internal affairs. On June 23, 2009, the President said this: "I've made it clear that the United States respects the sovereignty of the Islamic Republic of Iran, and is not interfering with Iran's affairs."

Later on, the President showed a bit more sympathy for the Iranian rebels' determination to toss out the mullahs, but still did not lend his moral authority to their cause.

Mr. Obama's words on Iran drove Senator McCain crazy, as they should have. I can't help but think that if the senator had displayed the same passion during his campaign in 2008 that he has shown regarding key issues in 2009, he might be the one facing down Iran, not Barack Obama.

Sen. John McCain (R-AZ, *center*), my pick as "Person of the Year" in 2009, speaks at a press conference on Capitol Hill regarding possible human rights sanctions against Iran. With him are Sen. Joseph Lieberman (I-CT, *left*) and Sen. Evan Bayh (D-IN, *right*).

But back to my original point—John McCain did not mount a full-court press campaign; he did not blitz his opponent. And he certainly did not use gadgets to his advantage. He ran a measured race and got his butt kicked because, as the senator found out, we are indeed living in a changing America. Machines now carry messages like lightning. The old-time methods of public discourse are pretty much a thing of the past.

There is some good news in all of this, however. When the tweets, Facebook updates, and YouTube videos subside, the folks seem to be still keeping an open mind about events. Thus, the modern guy, Mr. Obama, is now being evaluated based on performance, not some high-tech propaganda. This gives me hope. A President should rise and fall based on what he actually does, not what he *says*.

But back to *you*, the person who is reading this book. My God, how quaint is that?! You're holding an actual book and turning its pages. Relish the experience. It won't be long before that and many other things we have taken for granted become extinct, too. Very soon there'll be a machine that distills the knowledge in books so it can be fed intravenously into your brain without any work on your part. Yet another convenience that will rob us of personal creativity.

So the question becomes, what should you do in the face of great change?

Well, try this: don't you change unless it helps your life.

My "social networking" is done in person. I don't twitter. Or tweet, or whatever they call it. Also, I don't chat online, use an iPod, or rely on text messaging. I refuse to do these things because they do not help me. Let's take twittering, for example. Apparently, you use this medium to tell other people what you are doing all day, every day. But why? Why do you want folks to know your daily experiences? Does that help you in any way? Doesn't that take time away from other stuff that could advance your life, help you achieve something of value? I have asked some Twitter people why they do it, and the consensus is, "It's fun." Okay, fun is good as long as no one, including you, gets hurt. So if tweeting is entertaining for you, well, tweet hardy. For me, however, high-tech blathering is frittering away my time, which is already limited by a crowded work and home schedule.

I like to read. I learn things from reading books, magazines, and newspapers (God help me). I'm not sure I'd be learning a lot reading Taylor Swift's daily diary. As always, I could be wrong.

I also learn things from watching people and taking walks without headphones on. On these walks, I think and look at actual life. Machines are banned.

So how boring am I? Up there with Lawrence Welk, right? If you don't know old Lawrence, he was a bland bandleader whom your grandmother might have liked way back in the 1960s. Welk's big line was, "And a one and a two . . ." Stupefying.

Unlike Lawrence Welk, I am not boring on TV; at least, that's what the ratings and research indicate. Thank God, millions of folks think the presentation on *The O'Reilly Factor* is unique and spontaneous. That's because I actually think about what I'm going to do and say on the program. I think about this without Lady Gaga screaming in my ear, with all due respect to Ms. Gaga, a marketing genius.

Also, because I read an enormous amount, I am prepared to back up my opinions with actual facts. That separates me from many TV talking heads who spend hours in makeup with headphones on, bopping to the Crocodile Rock or something. Sorry if I sound supercilious, but I have not succumbed to the machine life. That, I believe, has helped me maintain success.

Sadly, it is hard to convince some younger folks that my strategy has merit. Compelling ideas come into clear minds. Walking in a forest or on a beach is good for clarity and creativity. Especially if you do this without Jay-Z (another marketing genius) rapping directly into your eardrum. Are you hearing me on this? Are you still able to hear?

The writer Stephen King recently wrote a novel in which cell phone users turned into violent zombies. He was obviously satirizing our machine-saturated society. But some folks actually are high-tech zombies in real life; they have lost the ability to experience reality. Want sex? You can get facsimile all over the Net. Want a date? You can chat up people all day long. Want food? Well, the Net can't feed you yet, but I'll bet they're working on it.

So let's return to the central question: How does a changing America directly affect you? The election of Barack Obama is illustration number one. He raised millions on the Net and convinced younger voters to support him in great numbers. Now, the President and his crew are affecting all of our lives. Without cyberspace, I do not believe an inexperienced politician like Obama would have been elected to the most powerful position in the world. Remember, Jimmy Carter and Bill Clinton had lengthy political résumés when they were elected. Barack Obama was a senator for less than two years, and did little of substance in his time on the Hill.

President Obama walks along the White House colonnade with his beloved BlackBerry!

The second change we all have to deal with is raising children. Have you tried having a conversation with a kid lately? It's never been easy, but these days it's a killer. Often, you have to literally yank portable machines out of their hands to get kids' attention. Predictably, the urchins resent the intrusion on their fun, so right away we adults are not in a great communication position.

Listen to this: according to a Kaiser Family Foundation study, American kids ages eight to eighteen spend 7.5 hours a day on average consuming electronic stimulation. Do the math. The kid sleeps nine hours, then goes to school for six. Therefore, Sally or Brendan has only 2.5 free hours a day unattached to machines. This is unbelievable. When do children play outside? When do they have conversations? If you think this isn't going to change the United States very soon, you're a Pinhead. This is BIG.

Here's the kid chart from Kaiser :

Watching TV	4.5 hours a day
Listening to music	2.5 hours a day
Talking on cell phones	30 minutes a day
Playing video games	1.3 hours a day
Text messaging	1.5 hours a day
Nonschool computer use	1.5 hours a day

Note that the chart's data accounts for the fact that each child has a different profile. Kaiser essentially pooled the information to come up with an average of total daily machine intrusion time. The numbers, of course, make the situation crystal clear: American children are hooked on tech, and the unintended consequences of that will radically change our society and country.

The Way We Were

In my house when I was growing up, we had a kitchen blender, a TV, and a few radios. Machine time was slim. Despite that, there wasn't much parent/kid chat, as I illustrated in my previous book, *A Bold Fresh Piece of Humanity*. At the nightly dinner table, my sister and I were held captive, since we had no escape from whatever my father and mother wanted to drop on us.

A sample conversation went like this:

Bill O'Reilly Sr.: These potatoes are great, aren't they? Why aren't you eating them, son?

Bill O'Reilly Jr.: Aren't these instant potatoes? They aren't real, are they, Mom?

Mom: There's no difference, honey.

Senior: Eat them, okay? Janet, you're not eating your potatoes, either.

Janet: Mmmmm.

Senior: Good peas, Mom. Kids, eat your peas.

Junior: Are these instant peas?

Senior: There's no such thing as instant peas. EAT THEM!

Junior [*points to Janet*]: She's not eating her peas. Why are you picking on me? It's not fair.

Senior: We don't waste food in this house! I want the potatoes and peas eaten.

Junior: I have to go to the bathroom.

Senior: You'll hold it until the potatoes and peas are gone.

Mom: Just eat up, kids, and then there's Oreos for dessert.

Junior: Mom, if you mix an Oreo with the peas, I might be able to eat them.

Senior: Don't be a wise guy. You know what happens to wise guys in this house.

Junior: Is it possible to be a wise girl? Janet's not eating anything.

Janet: Am, too.

Senior: That's enough. Eat your dinner. No more talking.

That kind of family interaction has made thousands of psycho-therapists wealthy.

Forty Years and Twenty-Eight Days Later

Now, let's fast-forward and listen to a contemporary family dinner conversation featuring Dad, Mom, Josh, and Abigail.

Dad: What's playing on your iPod, Abby?

Abby [*Bobs her head to the tune. She does not hear Dad.*]

Dad [*louder*]: Abby!

Abby [*looking up, annoyed*]: What? Can't you see I'm listening to my music, Dad?

Dad: What are you listening to?

Abby [*now looking really annoyed*]: Black Eyed Peas. Why?

Dad: Because it's impolite to listen to music at the table. Your mother and I would like to talk to you.

Abby: Why?

Dad: Josh, put that thing down!

Josh [*lowering his Nintendo DS, which features a fast-moving game in which guys blow each other up*]: Why?

Mom: Look, you two. We are having dinner as a family. This is family time.

Abby: I'm not hungry.

Josh: I'm not, either.

Dad: Well, you are still going to sit here and talk to us.

Abby: I have nothing to say.

Josh: I'm bored.

Dad: What did you do today, Abby?

Abby: Listened to music, texted my friends, played with my Wii.

Mom: How about you, Josh, what did you do?

Josh: Played *Madden NFL* on the computer, watched *G.I. Joe* on video, played with my DS.

Dad: Pass the potatoes.

My father passed away in 1986, and I cannot imagine him dealing with the high-tech age. He was a Depression-era kid and a naval officer during World War II; all of his experiences came from face-to-face human interaction. He even hated talking on the phone. In fact, I never saw my father on the phone for more than thirty seconds at a time unless he was yelling at some guy trying to sell him something. Then he took his time.

When I called home from El Salvador or Northern Ireland or someplace, he'd get on the line for about twenty seconds before inevitably saying, "Here's your mother."

By contrast, he'd sit on the patio in the summer and chat for hours with his friends. If he could see you, my father would talk to you.

Children today still respond to other children, but machines are curtailing their ability to converse and think creatively in person-to-person situations, as I have stated. Getting a verbal description beyond "cool" and "awesome" from a kid is no easy task for an adult. The truth is that children are bored with conversation because things aren't blowing up or rhyming (rap music). Again, this kind of youth life experience is changing America big-time, and few understand how it will eventually play out when today's kids become adults.

But one thing is virtually certain: Americans are losing the ability to think critically, and that will make it much easier for manipulative, charismatic politicians to gain power.

For parents and grandparents, the situation is frustrating because many of the things that we enjoyed in our youth are now obsolete and have been banished from society. Not good. Playground competition, creative game playing, Monopoly on rainy days—all of these things brought some maturity and a lot of joy, at least to me.

I've actually bribed kids to sample pond ice hockey, one-on-one basketball, and stickball against brick walls. For my trouble, I mostly get eye rolls and deep sighs. The machines are always calling these kids.

Sadly, there is little you can do about any of this, and truthfully, you shouldn't waste too much time trying to stem the tide. The kids will interact with machines, they will. But if you're a parent, design definite boundaries for your children about what they can and can't do in their free time. It will be tough, but you have to demand that they converse or at least listen to your words at the dinner table or elsewhere. Don't allow your children to become zombies dependent on cheap stimulation. These machines and the moronic stuff on them are addictive, and you, the parent, have an obligation to limit the stimulation in a fair way and keep your children clean.

Age-Old Wisdom

But things are not completely bleak. If you are articulate and well-read, your place in America is getting stronger no matter what age you are. If you know how to relate to people, how to engage them in conversation, your potential for prospering is greatly enhanced. With some hesitation, I'll use myself as an example.

I've been anchoring *The O'Reilly Factor* for fourteen years, and I am sixty-one years old. I keep myself in reasonable shape, but there is no question that I'm in the AARP zone. Years ago, I might have been pushed out by some hot-shot younger anchor. Remember, a younger Dan Rather (who turned out to be a Pinhead) replaced an older Walter Cronkite as the anchor of the *CBS Evening News* in March 1981. Cronkite was forced out of his job even though he was performing well. The CBS suits wrongly calculated that Rather would attract younger viewers and refresh the franchise. The result, as we now know, was disastrous. The *CBS Evening News* has never recovered.

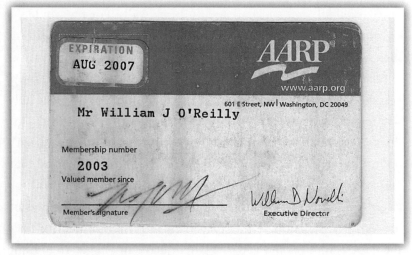

Here's proof that I'm a card-carrying member of the AARP, and proud of it!

But that most likely would not happen today. There are few hot-shot younger people in TV news now because their experience and education just can't measure up to those of us who worked in the golden age of network news.

Back in the 1970s and '80s, TV news was a serious business, and companies spent big money sending reporters around the globe to cover important stories. As a national correspondent for ABC News and, later, for *Inside Edition,* I traveled the world reporting all kinds of situations, including combat and intense political conflict. I have visited seventy-five countries and earned two master's degrees: one from Harvard's Kennedy School of Government, the other from Boston University's School of Communication. In addition, I spent my third year in college studying at the University of London in a third-year-abroad program. So which younger journalist is going to compete with that? You tell me.

These days, TV news outfits outsource just about everything. No longer is a Bill O'Reilly sent to Argentina to cover the Falkland Islands war. Now some guy named José from Buenos Aires will file the information. José is a lot cheaper, and that's primarily what news organizations care about these days.

Also, the decline of the disciplines of history and geography in America's public schools is shocking. Young journalists today often lack any knowledge of what happened before they showed up on the planet. Go out to the mall and ask some kid where Bangladesh is. Then ask the youth to name one Supreme Court justice. Try it.

So if you think about it, I'm pretty lucky. My competition for the anchor seat on the *Factor* is slim. The old adage says, "In the land of the blind, the one-eyed man is king." The rise of the machines is creating far more Pinheads than Patriots and is eroding the traditional skills needed to succeed in the communications industry. The strong will always survive, and if you are dependent on machines, rather than on your God-given abilities, you will not be strong. I suffered while building my frame of reference and experience file, but it is now rock solid. No machine is going to beat me in a debate.

In the future, a few citizens will dominate the many in America. Knowledge will be power, escapism will be weakness. Our society is indeed changing. All you can do is ride with it while sticking to your traditional disciplines. You'll win with those.

JELLY BEANS, PEANUTS, AND HUMBLE PIE

In December 2009 the Pew Research Center did a survey find-ing that Americans rated the first decade of the twenty-first century the worst in fifty years. Curiously, those polled rated the 1980s the best modern decade. Ronald Reagan presided in the White House for most of the '80s. More on that in a moment.

In addition to the Pew information, an ABC News poll found that a whopping 61 percent of Americans believe that the United States is in a long-term decline. To me, that proves that most of us are uneasy about the great changes taking place in America and around the world. We are not confident that the new age will help us very much or result in a more prosperous environment. We are concerned about our place in a changing America.

President Reagan succeeded in the 1980s because he successfully sold the vision of a strong, traditional America. He exuded confi-dence as he put forth that we are a noble nation whose blood and sacrifice have greatly benefited the world. Mr. Reagan was not a big details man while in the Oval Office. Rather, he was a symbol of America's strength and basic goodness. The bright, shining city on the hill image incisively defines the Reagan era.

Many liberal Americans despised President Reagan and still do. They claim that he ignored the poor and catered to the moneyed interests. They contend that his opposition to abortion demeaned women, while his intense dislike of runaway entitlement spending hurt the poor. That's the point here: Reagan's belief system is in sharp contrast with the policies of Barack Obama, and now the late President is used as a contrast magnet. Are you a Reagan person or an Obama person? And here is where America must make a major decision: go back to tradition in the Reagan mold, or continue with progressive change under the Obama banner.

Reagan versus Obama. That's what the next presidential election will likely be about. We just don't know who will be playing Reagan.

Former President Ronald Reagan will always be a true Patriot in my mind.

Can you imagine the newly elected Ron going to Cairo and telling the Muslim world that the USA had exploited them in the past? Can you imagine that? Even though America *has* exploited the Arab world at times, it has also greatly helped those politically challenged nations. Reagan would have trumpeted our largesse and avoided the mea culpas.

President Obama obviously sees it differently. He believes that a humble America will emerge as more powerful in world opinion than an arrogant America (Obama has branded the Bush administration as chief culprit in the hubris department). Mr. Obama's conciliatory demeanor abroad has played well with the liberal press, but back home the folks are becoming increasingly skeptical, especially when they hear statements like this:

> *The relationship between Islam and the West includes centuries of coexistence and cooperation, but also conflict and religious wars. More recently, tension has been fed by colonialism that denied rights and opportunities to many Muslims, and a Cold War in which Muslim-majority countries were too often treated as proxies without regard to their own aspirations.*

Ronald Reagan would have shuddered and said something like, "There you go again," the famous refrain from his presidential debate with Jimmy Carter. Unfortunately, in my *humble* opinion, President Obama has misread history. The primary oppressors of Muslims have been other Muslims. Few democratic states exist in the Islamic world. In fact, most are brutal totalitarian regimes where women are repressed and non-Muslims are persecuted. It's difficult to see what colonialism had to do with these cultural atrocities. Besides, the USA has never been involved with colonial activities in the Muslim world. With respect, Mr. Obama was talking through his hat in Cairo!

If you understand America, you know that most Americans sincerely believe that their country is a force for good in the world. And you know what? It is. I've seen it time and time again. For all his unilateral bluster, President Bush saved millions of lives in Africa by financing a number of AIDS and malaria projects. Because of the tens of millions of dollars he spent on those programs, compliments of the American taxpayer, many human beings are alive today. That's just one small example of what the USA routinely practices all around the world. Whenever disaster hits, we as individuals and as a nation are the most generous responders. Just ask the Haitians.

So President Obama risks damage to his image when he runs

down the USA. He is far too smart a man not to understand historical reality. I can only assume that portraying America in a more humble way overseas is a strategy on his part. It is the only thing I can think of that would drive such rhetoric. Whatever his motivation, it is a Pinhead move.

Psychoanalyzing anyone is a waste of time, so I will pose just one more question about Barack Obama's personal worldview. Speaking at a press conference in April 2010, he told the world that, "like it or not," America is a superpower. Some liberals I know don't like it. They see the USA as a bully. But I agree with many of our fellow citizens that America's superpower status is often a force for good. Our military and humanitarian strength has brought relief to millions. Every tyrant in the world fears us. After every disaster, Americans are on the ground, helping out. We are an overwhelmingly positive presence in this world because we have the money and power to impose justice and to finance charity.

Portugal is a nice country; can they do that?

And if the United States does not right wrongs, who will? China? Russia? Uganda?

The question then becomes this: Is President Obama comfortable in his role as the most powerful person in the world? After closely observing him, I believe that he likes personal power, but is a bit uneasy with macro-power. I could be wrong on this.

Although younger Americans are not as emotional about their country as previous generations, most of us still admire a strong leader who talks *up* the USA. Ronald Reagan was a genius at it. Barack Obama has not yet embraced the concept. But why not?

The reason, I think, is that the President believes America is fundamentally flawed, and that we need to be more progressive in our outlook to create a more just society. Right now, the evidence suggests that Mr. Obama's "change you can believe in" mantra is being driven by his core belief that our system isn't fair because it is stacked against the poor and disadvantaged. Therefore, the President wants to expand government power in order to provide folks with what they need: health care, fewer carbon fuels, and a more diverse economy that shares wealth.

In addition, Barack Obama is an internationalist, which means he believes America does not have an "exceptional" place in the world. He wants the United States to be humble on the international front, and if that means overemphasizing his country's mistakes, so be it.

The Reagan vision, of course, was the exact opposite: smaller government, lower federal taxes, expanded opportunities for the private marketplace in order to drive job creation in the private sector. President Reagan believed in the "trickle-down theory"—that is, if corporate America is doing well, the workingman and -woman will benefit by more employment opportunities and increased salaries produced by competition.

Also, Mr. Reagan believed, like his acolytes today (e.g., Dick Cheney), that the United States has an obligation to lead the world toward more freedom. In the eyes of conservatives, we are not one nation among many—we are the righteous world leader.

But as President Obama implied in that April press conference, being a superpower means we get dragged into everybody else's problems. That can be very painful, as we found out in Vietnam and Iraq. Some conservatives, like Pat Buchanan, believe it is insane to be the world's beat cop.

Today in America, progressives are center stage, and they tend to focus on "social justice," not international justice. The massive domestic spending embraced by the Obama administration in pursuit of helping less affluent Americans has created fear in the financial community. Like ultraliberal California, the USA could go bankrupt if entitlement spending continues to expand. And the folks sense it.

It would be easy to write that Ronald Reagan was a Patriot and Barack Obama is a Pinhead. That, however, would be a pure ideological opinion because the data is not yet complete. President Obama's mandate for progressive change is not going well, but as history demonstrates, things can change fast.

So let's say something more nuanced: both Obama and Reagan can be considered Patriots for their public service alone. Also, President Reagan's *accomplishments* put him firmly in Patriot territory, while President Obama's achievements, so far, cannot be defined. It's simply too early in his term. But, no question, Mr. Obama has already entered the land of the Pinhead on a few occasions, and the health care deal is a huge gamble with the country's future. Patriotic Americans have a right to be extremely skeptical about the President's overall vision for America. That being said, true Patriots are always fair-minded and should give the President a case-by-case hearing. When things don't add up, like the exploding budget deficit, let him know it. That's what the Tea Party movement is all about.

But when Americans see the President's policy of attacking the al-Qaeda leadership with drone-driven missiles working very well, we should also acknowledge that.

It is true, however, that there comes a time when an overall assessment has to be made of a leader. That day of reckoning may spell very bad news for Barack Obama. Because so many of his policies have been Far Left leaning, he is close to the point of no return unless the economy begins to soar.

Because America remains a Center-Right country, I will make this prediction: if President Obama does not move rightward toward the center, there will be trouble ahead for him on a number of fronts. We are living in a dangerous time. Outwitting our enemies will take strength and smarts. President Obama is smart, but is he tough enough to defeat evil? Will the Chicago community organizer be able to set aside his liberal inclinations and do what is necessary both to protect America and also put it back on solid financial footing? These are the vital questions.

Historically, liberal policies have not led to financial discipline nor have they instilled fear in belligerent tyrants. I guess there is always a first time, but you might be a Pinhead to bet on it. Come back to the traditional center way of governing, Mr. President, or risk being a one-term guy. Already, some are saying that the Democratic Party is self-destructing, even as it should be enjoying the apex of its power. *New York Times* columnist David Brooks put it this way:

> The [Democratic Party] is led by insular liberals from big cities and the coasts, who neither understand nor sympathize with moderates. . . .
> We're only in the early stages of the liberal suicide march but already there have been three phases. First, there was the stimulus package . . . [that] Congressional Democrats used as a pretext to pay for $787 billion worth of pet programs with borrowed money. . . .
> Then there is the budget. Instead of allaying moderate anxieties about the deficits, the budget is expected to increase the government debt by $11 trillion between 2009 and 2019.
> Finally, there is health care. . . . The bills do almost nothing to control health care inflation. . . . They do little to reward efficient providers and reform inefficient ones.

Although Mr. Brooks is a moderate (conservative by the über-liberal *Times* standards), he is obviously chiding the Democratic congressional leadership for being too liberal and out of touch with the folks. The American people, however, are not likely to make a distinction between the White House and Congress. The huge debt run-up, the health care fiasco, and the dubious war on terror strategy are happening on Obama's watch. He will be held responsible if things go south, no matter how much of the chaos was caused by the fools on Capitol Hill. If the President does not want to be infected by the Pinhead contagion that is now rampant in Washington, he must begin to take a few non–Far Left positions on vital issues. If he doesn't, the strong current of voter disenchantment will eventually send him floating off into the sunset.

Just ask Jimmy Carter.

★

CHAPTER 5

The Boston Massacre

THE STORM CLOUD HOVERING over President Obama in late 2009 was nothing compared to what arrived early the next year. The pounding he took on Tuesday, January 19, 2010, should have given him brain freeze. On that blustery day in Massachusetts, some of the most liberal voters in the country elected a Republican to replace the late Edward Kennedy in the Senate. It was absolutely astonishing.

You know the story. Democrat Martha Coakley was ahead by 30 points in the polls after she won the primary. But as events unfolded in the autumn of '09, things began to totter, and four days before the vote, Ms. Coakley found herself behind in a Suffolk University poll. By the way, the extremely liberal *Boston Globe* ignored the stunning poll upon its release. And the *Globe* wonders why it's going bankrupt.

With Coakley's support cracking, a dramatic call was made

to the bullpen. Look up in the sky—it's a bird, it's a plane, it's AIR FORCE ONE! Two days before the vote, the Eagle had landed in Boston; President Obama had arrived to save Martha Coakley.

Only he didn't.

Republican state senator Scott Brown defeated Coakley by 100,000 votes. For the first time in almost fifty years, Massachusetts had elected a GOPer to the Senate. And not just any Republican. Brown said flat out that he would try to block ObamaCare if elected, and that he would oppose almost all the President's big-spending policies. In other words, Brown didn't run against Ms. Coakley; he ran against Obama.

Hot off the presses! Senator-elect Scott Brown (R-MA) holds up a *Boston Herald* newspaper announcing his historic victory in Massachusetts.

Days after the shocking vote, *Time* magazine put Barack Obama on its cover with the headline: NOW WHAT?

Good question.

Some partisan Pinheads on cable TV attacked Scott Brown by

calling him vile names and smearing those who voted for him even though many of them had supported Barack Obama for President just a few months prior. The reaction to Brown's victory by some on the Far Left was downright ugly. It makes one wonder whether these people are simply damaged emotionally. The voters of Massachusetts were clearly sending a message to the rest of the country. By insulting that message, the radical Left just made more enemies, as if they don't already have enough. We're not talking about shooting yourself in the foot here, radical Left people; we're talking about blowing your brains out.

But let's return to the real world and leave Far Left loon land behind. What *exactly* was the Bay State message, anyway?

Actually, it was quite Patriotic in the great tradition of Massachusetts. I believe that most Americans, including many liberals, do not trust the federal government. I mean, we have to put up with it because that's our system, but do you really think the giant, chaotic apparatus in Washington can bring success and happiness to your life? Anyone who believes that should travel to Havana, Cuba, and take a look around.

No, most Americans want to pursue happiness without Uncle Sam making things more difficult for them. And in the beginning of 2010, that was exactly what the federal government was doing: making things worse for hardworking Americans. Only Far Left, Kool-Aid-drinking Pinheads failed to notice.

MEDIC ALERT

The economy was the best example. With unemployment at 10 percent and workers insecure almost everywhere, the folks were in no mood for the vast expansion of the federal government. To be fair, the bad economy was not Barack Obama's fault, and not even Moses could have healed the economic breach in a year. But the President insisted on spending incredible amounts of taxpayer money to prop up failing companies and state governments and had little to show for it. The voters in Massachusetts clearly noticed.

Then there was federal health care reform, or ObamaCare. As we discussed, Yale PhD candidates had troubling figuring it out. Every time Nancy Pelosi wailed about a "public option," folks began swearing under their breath. "What the deuce is a public option? What are you talking about, lady?" The health care debate was so strident and complicated that it simply wore many Americans out.

A SAFE ASSUMPTION

By the time the underwear terrorist appeared on Christmas Day (just a few weeks before the vote in Massachusetts), it appears that the folks had had enough. When the Obama administration announced that the jihadist loon they had apprehended would be allowed to lawyer up in Michigan, the swearing became audible. Once again, a foreign terrorist trying to kill American civilians had been granted the full rights of an American citizen, rather than being handed over to military authorities and "debriefed" by them without Mr. Miranda in the room. Polls showed most Americans thought the move by Attorney General Eric Holder was incredibly dumb.

An interesting footnote: while some pundits attributed Brown's victory primarily to the economy and health care, his campaign's internal polling showed that many who voted for him did so because they objected to Obama's somewhat "soft" approach to the war on terror.

And that perception worsened when the President's top security guys told a congressional committee they had not even been *consulted* about interrogating the underwear bomber. If *that* story had broken before the Brown-Coakley vote, old Scott might have won by a half million votes.

So the handwriting was incredibly clear one year into President Obama's term: THINGS WERE NOT GOING WELL! The committed left-wing press, however, remained in denial.

The *Boston Globe* editorialized: "Brown's strong win does not negate the resounding mandate that President Obama and the Democrats received in 2008."

Are you kidding me? The President directly appealed to the voters of Massachusetts to reinforce his "mandate," and they answered, absolutely not. Paging the *Boston Globe* editorial team. Does the word *Pinheads* mean anything to you?

The *Washington Post* was almost as bad. It editorialized, "We don't believe that Tuesday's defeat means Mr. Obama should back away from his goal of expanding access to health care while controlling health care costs."

The day after that editorial, Speaker of the House Nancy Pelosi told the nation she did not have the votes to pass ObamaCare "at this time." But as it turned out, a combination of big-money deals to various states and the President's high-profile determination reversed the course of mandated national health care.

So it is still an open question as to whether or not the concerns that drove the Massachusetts stunner will spread nationwide, causing Democrats to replace the Republicans as the party of no (as in "No, we are not going to vote for you"). We'll see.

History, of course, has a way of intruding on pundits like me; events can overtake analysis, making us look like Pinheads. But I will speak my piece on this anyway: Barack Obama is a gambler. He took a big chance with health care reform and didn't fold 'em when Kenny Rogers might have. His grit in sticking with something he believes in is admirable. Nevertheless, I continue to believe that ObamaCare will not serve the country well. Why? Because the massive health care entitlement is far too expensive and confusing. In the interest of Patriotism, let me elaborate on some of the solutions I suggested earlier to solve this incredible mess.

The federal government should have passed tort reform so that doctors and other medical personnel could protect themselves against frivolous lawsuits generated by greedy lawyers who know how to game the system. In Great Britain, if a judge deems that a lawsuit has little or no merit, the guy who sues pays all costs.

The feds should also allow all health insurance companies to compete nationwide. This free-market approach would undercut pricing and possibly introduce more options to the people.

On the other hand, I do believe the feds should impose standards of behavior on health insurance companies and fine the hell out of them when they fail to pay a legitimate claim or throw a client off the rolls because he or she gets hurt or becomes sick. Therefore, I have no problem with that part of the ObamaCare legislation.

The overall law, however, chills me, and I am not alone. Creating another monstrous bureaucracy that will spend—and possibly misuse—trillions of dollars is not in the best interest of the nation. If we go under financially, every American will pay a huge price. And there is no cure for national bankruptcy.

WHAT'S MINE IS YOURS

The final word on national health care reform is that, even if the law turns out to be a disaster, our legislative system worked. The debate was brutal. Both sides slugged it out for months while the nation watched and gathered information. Because the Democrats controlled Congress, ObamaCare finally squeaked through, but it was straight-razor close, and there were more than a few nicks when the shave was done. All in all, it was a good fight. There were Patriots and Pinheads galore, of course. Depending on your point of view, you can tag them. But I like the fact that Americans know the issues and now understand the stark differences between liberals and conservatives, Democrats and Republicans. There is no fog anymore.

President Obama wants the feds to impose "social justice." He wants Washington to amass as much power as it can, so states that do not embrace the entitlement culture will be forced to do so by the federal government.

That's what Barack Obama's true mission is. He wants to level the playing field and narrow the gap between the affluent and those who don't have much. Is the President a Pinhead because of his belief system? No! He sincerely believes America should be a nation that provides for those who do not have. I won't designate someone a Pinhead for well-thought-out, sincerely held beliefs, even if I think they are misguided.

But Mr. Obama *is* a Pinhead when you think about the way in which he attained power. During his presidential campaign, he ran as a moderate, a man who wanted to change the country for the better but in a pragmatic, nonideological way. Well, that posture has turned out to be a ruse. Barack Obama is the most liberal President I've seen in my lifetime. In fact, he may well be the most left-wing chief executive in American history. That doesn't make him an eternal Pinhead, but it does cast doubt on his honesty. Few understood the extent of his liberalism when they voted for him. Now we know.

★

CHAPTER 6

The Audacity of Dopes:
Colossal Pinheads in Our Midst

THE TRUE PINHEADS of the world can be found in the precincts of betrayal, abuse of power, apathy toward the suffering of others, greed, envy, and exploitation of the powerless. As I've written, we all are Pinheads on occasion, but if we live without standards, we risk being Pinheads all the time.

Most of the people that I know are good people, and many of them have trouble understanding the cruelty that we all witness in our lives. How can so-and-so do that? they ask. Well, the answer is kind of simple and very important. Many human beings put their own self-interest ahead of everything else. If they want something, they'll do what they have to do to get it. When confronted with their heinous activities, the self-involved often retreat into a dark world. The religious writer Sarah Young puts it this way: "Man's tendency is to hide from his sin, seeking refuge in the darkness.

There he indulges in self-pity, denial, self-righteousness, blaming, and hatred."

Out of that emotional grouping, rationalizations are easy to form. Excuses for bad behavior are everywhere. Look, I do this myself. Whenever I commit some stupid or sinful act, my first instinct is to attempt to explain away my Pinheaded behavior. But I've come to the point in my life where I stop that nonsense quickly. We are all sinners; to spend time trying to justify the sin just makes it worse. Own it and try not to do it again. If you have to make restitution, make it. True Pinheads will never get that simple rule. That's why they are true Pinheads.

NEWSWORTHY CEOS?

Sometimes, the Pinheads manage to achieve power, which makes them especially annoying and sometimes even dangerous. Here's a vivid example. There's a media guy named Jeff Zucker who runs the National Broadcasting Corporation. Early in his career, Zucker was a creative type. As a producer, he helped build *The Today Show* into the powerhouse it remains today. From very early on, Zucker had a good relationship with Katie Couric, which many speculate helped him rise in the company.

Then, as often happens, Zucker was promoted and given immense power by General Electric boss Jeffrey Immelt, whom I flayed in my previous book. GE owns NBC, and Immelt allowed Zucker to run wild, nearly ruining the NBC brand and absolutely devastating many lives.

Zucker is the man who scheduled Jay Leno at 10:00 P.M. because NBC's prime-time lineup was so weak, thanks to Zucker, that he had little else to put on the air. Poor Jay. He was thrown up against high-rated dramas like *CSI* and got his butt kicked all over the place.

Desperate to save his own butt, Zucker put Leno back on at

11:30, which resulted in a very public dispute and the ultimate firing of Conan O'Brien. Because of the chaos that Zucker imposed, hundreds of people were adversely affected. But Zucker's the kind of guy who is in it for the power, so if you have to die (figuratively speaking) for his sake, then you have to die. As long as his rear end is saved, everyone else is expendable. That, of course, is standard management behavior in corporate America; it's not unique to Zucker.

But what does make Jeff Zucker a monumental Pinhead is what he did at NBC News. The culture of that place had been liberal for years, but Tom Brokaw and Brian Williams tamped the lefty stuff down on the air. *The Today Show* was mostly Left but, again, they weren't in your face about it, at least not most of the time.

NBC News, however, developed a big problem. Their cable news outfit, MSNBC, was failing even after hundreds of millions of dollars had been invested in it. NBC's cable news partner, the Microsoft Corporation, was appalled. After all, Fox News, which started up a few months after MSNBC in 1996, was far more successful, making tons of money. So what the heck was going on? Microsoft wanted to know.

Emerging from his lair, Jeff Zucker had no answers. Then, kind of suddenly, good fortune smiled on him in the form of an energetic politician named Barack Obama.

Sensing some destiny in play, Zucker and his underlings decided to drop any pretense of reporting the news and get into the business of using MSNBC to promote left-wing causes—causes like the candidacy of one Senator Obama.

It is worth pausing here to deal with an inevitable criticism of my analysis. Some Americans, as mentioned before, believe that Fox News is an arm of the Republican machine, that my employer is in business to promote the Grand Old Party. I have always found that belief strange. Yes, FNC has a number of conservative commentators who certainly vote Republican most of the time. It is also true that we have hired guys like Newt Gingrich and Karl Rove to do political analysis. But we also have committed Democrats like Lanny Davis, Geraldine Ferraro, and Joe Trippi on board. In addition, you may remember that I and a number of other FNC commentators hammered John McCain during the campaign. In fact, as I recalled earlier, the senator loathed coming on the *Factor*, because we gave him no quarter. I asked him the hardest questions I could think of.

That was quite a contrast to Zucker's operation, which openly rooted for Barack Obama to win the election. I mean, it was stunning to watch. The network's new ad campaign, inviting viewers to "experience the power of change," echoing Obama's own campaign message, was just the tip of things. Because MSNBC has no news correspondents, it relies on NBC network correspondents for information. So people like Andrea Mitchell and Lester Holt, two experienced reporters, had to appear on a network that was actually campaigning for the Democratic candidate. That had never happened before in media history. You have to hope that God in heaven protected Chet Huntley and John Chancellor from seeing that abomination.

Clearly, I'm not the only one to call out Jeff Zucker. Here the NBC Universal CEO fires back at comedian Jon Stewart, saying it was "unfair" and "absurd" for the funnyman to question CNBC's coverage of the financial news.

But it gets worse. Not only did MSNBC programming violate every journalistic rule of fairness, Zucker also hired a bunch of guttersnipes who proceeded to smear Republicans and conservatives by launching vicious personal attacks. Broadcast journalism had never seen anything like this. There were absolutely no rules. These hired verbal assassins took rank propaganda from Far Left Web sites and broadcast it as truth. They used vile gossip and innuendo to smear John McCain, Sarah Palin, and anyone who supported them. Disgraceful doesn't even begin to cover it.

All the while, Jeff Zucker was at the helm. He's quite a guy.

During the presidential campaign, MSNBC's prime time got a small increase in audience, primarily people heavily invested in Barack Obama. But a year after Mr. Obama's election, MSNBC had lost most of that audience and was once again a ratings and editorial embarrassment.

No decent executive (or person, for that matter) would allow what passes for programming at MSNBC. Yes, the individuals who traffic in the personal attacks are responsible for their slander. But the architect of the smear machine is Jeff Zucker, who should watch out, because if the old saying is true, what goes around, comes around.

EPIDEMIC NONSENSE

There are a number of folks such as Minister Louis Farrakhan, the Reverend Jeremiah Wright, Bill Moyers, Michael Savage, David Duke, et al. who are Pinheads and there's no doubt about it. But these are obvious, easy targets that don't much advance the cultural dialogue.

I must say, however, that Farrakhan sometimes amuses me. I don't mean his insane ramblings about "wicked Jews." That kind of vile stuff is simply unacceptable. But occasionally the guy is so out there that I can't help but laugh at the insanity. Yes, you can call me a Pinhead for doing this.

But here's a good example of the stuff I'm talking about. Remember the brief swine flu scare in 2009? Well, Farrakhan seized upon that to say, "The Earth can't take 6.5 billion people. We just can't feed that many. So what are we going to do? Kill as many as you can. We have to develop a science that kills them and makes it look as though they died from some disease."

It looks like Nation of Islam Minister Louis Farrakhan is
making a point of saying something Pinheaded again here!

So according to Minister Farrakhan, the swine flu is some man-made doomsday bug.

The man's a complete Pinhead. Can you believe thousands of people pay money to hear his speeches? Every one of those people—every one of them—is a Pinhead, too.

LEGALLY BLIND

We have witnessed some confounding Pinhead moves in our time, but every once in a while, something happens in America that makes me doubt my country, which is painful for any Patriot. It's kind of like what the priest pedophilia scandal did to some Roman Catholics: it made them question the validity of their own church.

On March 3, 2006, Marine Lance Corporal Matthew Snyder, just twenty years old, was killed in Iraq when the Humvee he was riding in went off the road and rolled over. A week later, the funeral for Matthew was held in his hometown of Westminster, Maryland.

Outside the church, a group of insane fanatics calling themselves the Westboro Baptist Church picketed. They chanted ugly things about Matthew and other American military people killed in action. They claimed that God directly caused Matthew's death because the United States "accepts" gay people. They believe that the deity is punishing America because homosexuality is "tolerated."

This vile group has been around for years, but this time someone stood up to them. Matthew's father, Albert, filed a federal lawsuit against Westboro's leader, Fred Phelps, and his organization. Mr. Snyder stated that the group intentionally inflicted emotional distress on him and his family, invaded their privacy, and was guilty of a civil conspiracy.

A trial commenced, and in October 2007 a jury found Phelps and his "church" guilty, awarding the Snyder family nearly $11 million in damages. The judge in the trial, Richard Bennett, lowered the verdict to $5 million, but a satisfying judgment was in hand. Not for long, though.

Westboro appealed to the Fourth Circuit in Virginia, and three judges—Robert King, Dennis Shedd, and Allyson Duncan—overturned the guilty verdict on the grounds that what the fanatics did wasn't bad enough! The judges wrote, "Although reasonable people may disagree about the appropriateness of the Phelps protest, this conduct simply does not satisfy the heavy burden required for the tort of intentional infliction of emotional distress under Maryland law."

Are you kidding me? These judges believe there could be a debate about the *appropriateness of the protest*? Really? Just what exactly is appropriate about screaming that God murdered a marine because his country won't persecute homosexuals? Who exactly is going to defend that position . . . Satan?

The legal travesty those judges created is what I mean when I talk about being PINHEADS. Amazingly, two of these judges were appointed by President George W. Bush, so they're not left-wing loons. They just live in a world of words on paper. Lawbook Land. They are incapable of understanding true justice because they believe it occurs only in word form. Can you imagine any intelligent person writing that there could be an honest debate over the vicious actions of the Westboro nuts? It's impossible in the real world. But not in Lawbook Land.

Then the judges made the awfulness even worse.

Stunning all fair-minded people, they ruled that the Snyder family actually had to pay the Westboro loons more than $16,000 in court costs. At first I thought the judges had been compelled to do that by law after overturning a judgment. But no, it was a discretionary decision. On the *Factor,* attorney and Fox News anchor Megyn Kelly sided with the judges, explaining that it is "customary" for the loser of an appeal to pay the winner. Megyn further explained that Al Snyder was late in objecting to the judge's ruling (Snyder's attorney denies that), so you can't blame the judges.

I can't blame the judges? Of course I can. They made the wrong call on appeal and rubbed the Snyder family's faces in it. Talk about cruel and unusual punishment! The interruption of the funeral was an extreme case of blatant wrongdoing. It's not some run-of-the-mill civil beef. A man's son is killed, and vile people mock his death at the funeral? And judges who have the power to punish that action do not? And then actually reward the evildoers? Where are we . . . in North Korea?

Megyn Kelly thinks I'm a Pinhead because I don't consider legal precedent, and she's right, I don't. The three federal judges did not *have* to charge the Snyder family court costs. But they did. I don't give a damm about three robes hiding behind law journals. They did the wrong thing, morally. They could have legally set aside the court cost issue, but they did not.

Reasonable people may disagree about the appropriateness of the court's action, to borrow some of the most stupid words I've ever heard from a judge. And I do disagree.

There comes a time when American judges should simply do the conscionable thing. Our justice system was designed to right wrongs, but Pinheads who often see themselves as guardians of the legal gate pervert that intent.

Still believing in the American system, the Snyder family is taking the case to the Supreme Court, where I am hopeful reason and justice will prevail. There is no question that Phelps and his thugs wanted to hurt the Snyders and all other military families. If the judges don't get that, they should resign. There is a right and a wrong here, and the Fourth Circuit Court of Appeals embraced the wrong.

By the way, I offered to pay the Snyder's court costs should the system come knocking on their door. I simply will not let this injustice stand without some kind of response.

And there's one final note that I want to send directly to Judges King, Shedd, and Duncan. When told the Snyder family did not have enough cash to pay the court costs, Westboro's evil pastor, Fred Phelps, told the press that the family could cover the expense out of Matthew Snyder's federal death benefits. How does *that* sit with you, federal judges?

HUME-AND-KINDNESS HATERS

Sometimes the debate over whether a person is a Pinhead or a Patriot gets complicated, and such was the case after my Fox News colleague Brit Hume delivered some advice to the scandal-ridden golfer Tiger Woods.

The Hume-Woods confrontation began when Brit, speaking on FNC in his capacity as an analyst, said this about the golfer.

Brit Hume: He's said to be a Buddhist. I don't think that faith offers the kind of forgiveness and redemption that is offered by the Christian faith. So my message to Tiger would be "Tiger, turn to the Christian faith and you can make a total recovery and be a great example to the world."

Well, you would have thought Mr. Hume had recommended devil worship to Mr. Woods rather than forgiving introspection. The Far Left press went wild, branding Hume a religious fanatic who was trying to impose his belief system not only on Tiger Woods but on *everybody*. MSNBC and the *Washington Post* led the gnashing of teeth.

In response the conservative *Washington Times* editorialized:

> *If there were any doubt that much of the media is hostile to traditional Christianity, that doubt has been drowned in the wake of a vicious verbal assault on FNC's Brit Hume after comments he made about Tiger Woods. The histrionic fulminations against Hume for his inoffensive expression of faith expose an ugly strain of anti-religious bigotry that is spreading inside this country's liberal establishment.*

On the *Factor*, I interviewed Hume, who denied he was pros-
elytizing and said he was simply giving Tiger Woods advice that he
believed might help him.

I know Brit Hume and believe him. He meant no harm, and certainly his advice falls under the definition of legitimate commentary.
Yes, Brit is a committed Christian, but so what? He correctly stated
that in Buddhism there is no emphasis on redemption, because there
is no concept of "sin." He also clearly explained the Christian tenet of
forgiveness and the relief that concept might bring a person caught
up in indiscretions. Finally, Tiger Woods is free to take or leave any
advice offered, so what's the big deal?

Despite my stated logic, some good people disagreed with Brit,
placing him in the Pinhead category. I received thousands of e-mails
on the subject.

Nancy, who lives in Connecticut, wrote, "Religion is such a
deeply personal issue that I feel making a discussion topic of someone's belief system is wrong. If Mr. Hume wanted to reach out to
Tiger Woods, he should have done so privately."

William from Alaska put forth this: "I was shocked by Brit
Hume's tirade. His favoring Christianity over Buddhism is uncon-
scionable. Mr. Hume has proven himself a bigot."

Gary, who resides in New York City, also was disenchanted: "Fox
News Channel is no place for that kind of 'advice' from a respected
newsman. Wrong place, wrong subject, wrong time. I think you
should have nailed him on that, Bill."

But why, Gary? Brit was doing exactly what he gets paid to do,
give his opinion. In this case, the analysis was theologically based,
but again, why the angst? Tiger Woods had major trouble in his life.
The discussion was about how the man might mitigate that trouble.
Brit Hume simply gave him an option.

So in my opinion, Brit was not, in that case, a Pinhead. I do
understand, however, how some folks might think that he deni-
grated Buddhism, certainly a legitimate religion. My analysis is that

Brit simply stated one big difference between Christianity and Buddhism and how the former might help Mr. Woods in the forgiveness realm. Brit was putting forth his theory and opinion, which he is certainly entitled to do.

Brit Hume isn't the only Fox News person who folks are cheering for and against!

The critics of Brit Hume fall into two basic categories: those who believe he overstepped the analysis line and bashed Buddhism, and those who think he has no right even to mention a Christian solution to a complicated problem.

The Buddhism critics have a legitimate point of discussion, so they are Patriots for speaking their minds. The Christian objection smacks of censorship and bias, so those who embrace it are Pinheads.

As for Brit Hume, he took the heat, articulated his case, and didn't back down. He also bears no malice toward those who criticized him. So he's a Patriot.

It comes down to this: it is always Patriotic to stick up for your core beliefs, as Brit Hume did. But some of his critics, who were sincere in their dissent toward what he said, were also sticking up for their beliefs. So even though disagreement was in the air, so was Patriotism on both sides.

But those who hammered Hume in personal ways, trying to brand him as a fanatic or worse, are obviously Pinheads. Thanks to Brit Hume and Tiger Woods, a central theme of this book has now been stated: Pinheads try to harm people with whom they disagree; they want to punish and demean them.

Patriots, on the other hand, respect robust debate and have the courage to state their beliefs without rancor. Think about people you know in your life, and think about yourself.

Where do you stand?

★

It's All About Me

O'Reilly, I love you, man. But shut up once in a while.
                                    —*Yankee Stadium spectator*

MANY AMERICANS THINK that I, your humble correspondent, am one of the biggest Pinheads in the country. When there is no malice behind the thought, I am amused by the description. When there is malice, I have to wonder, Why do some folks want to stick pins in my head as if I'm some wild voodoo *houngan* trying to scare gullible folks into giving him money?

After fourteen years of anchoring the *Factor*, I am used to the slings and arrows. They whiz in nearly every day. Thank God for my pal Glenn Beck. Since he arrived at Fox News, he's taken some of the heat off me. But still, there is no question that I remain one of the most controversial men in the country. Again, why?

THE CONFIDENCE FACTOR

The answer lies partly in a trait that President Obama and I have in common. We both deliver our messages with confidence. I can't tell you how many letters I've received calling me arrogant after I've stated a strong opinion on something. For what action, I ask, am I deemed arrogant? The answer usually comes down to style, not substance. Because I state my case with certainty, some believe I am supercilious, a person who thinks he knows more than anyone else. Occasionally President Obama comes off that way as well, does he not?

So am I a Pinhead for exuding confidence while analyzing the news? Here's a shocker: *I don't think so.* I base my opinions on solid research and deliver my Talking Points memo with the authority of experience and knowledge. If I stumbled around looking unsure and hesitant, if I based my opinions on what I thought an ideological audience wanted to hear, could I honestly run a no-spin zone? No, I could not. I'd have to work for NBC News.

One of the reasons that President Bush lost the locker room midway through his second term was that he seemed tentative on vital subjects like Iraq and Hurricane Katrina. The President did not seem to have control of the situations, and voters quickly picked up on that. For Mr. Bush, verbal presentations were not easy. Obviously, he is not a glib man. So he often came across as shaky when an authoritative posture was needed in order to sow confidence.

Back in the mid-1990s, I was studying at Harvard's Kennedy School of Government (just *that* makes me arrogant in the eyes of some). Seeking a class that I might be able to use in real life, I signed up for a course on persuasion. The professor was a Pinhead, but in a good way. He was a guy who mostly lived in his own mind, constantly mulling over ideas and theories. But he was a brilliant thinker.

The professor taught me that to truly persuade another person who is opposed to your ideas, you not only have to make stronger arguments, you also have to be able to convince your skeptical opponent that you are in command of the situation. To be persuaded, a person has to submit. And most Americans are not submissive types. But we can be won over if we believe a person is sincere and has ideas that can better our own personal situations.

Does the name Barack Obama ring a bell? Isn't that what he did in the presidential campaign? He persuaded 53 percent of the voters to pull the lever on his behalf. And he did it almost entirely on personal charisma, because he had no real record to run on.

But back to me (how arrogant is that phrase?). I differ from the President because I do not seek approval. I state my case and let the chips fall. I want you to think about what we on the *Factor* are putting out there, but I don't expect agreement. I mean, I'm happy when that happens, but it is not mandatory. In fact, I respect people like Megyn Kelly who energetically disagree with me on some issues now and then. That's *fun* for me.

So I am not getting the arrogant deal. Am I overbearing? Sometimes. Obnoxious? Of course. Impatient with Pinheads who won't answer direct questions? All day long.

Look, I took a chance with this *Factor* no-spin concept. In fact, it was a huge gamble. I could have made millions simply reading the news and interviewing people with standard questions like: "Tell me more." But how boring is that?

As an American who tries to be Patriotic, I was sick of TV news phonies who were afraid to say anything controversial. "Thanks so much," the media Pinheads wail. "Great to see you!" Yeech.

So I decided to *do* something about it and designed the *Factor* in Cambridge, Massachusetts, in between my Harvard classes. The concept was simple because, as you may know, I am a simple man. I set up some rules to define an original TV news/analysis program. Please read them and decide whether I'm a Pinhead or Patriot.

TAKING THE PATRIOT CHALLENGE

Rule One: Tell the truth, always.

Rule Two: Insist on the question being answered. If necessary re-ask it a number of times, and always tell the viewer why you are repeating yourself. In other words, if the guest decides to dance, step on his or her toes.

Rule Three: Interrupt. This is the most controversial rule of all. President Obama often filibusters his way through interviews. His answers are so lengthy you could have a pizza delivered in that time. In that way, he controls the conversation, avoiding follow-up questions and debate. You may have noticed that *never* happens in the no-spin zone. I simply cut people off if they wander or repeat themselves. Is that obnoxious? Of course it is. Do I get nasty mail when I do that? Of course I do. But it has to be done if I don't want to waste your time. And I don't.

Rule Four: Admit you're wrong when you are actually wrong, and cede a point when your guest makes a valid argument. That's the right thing to do and makes the debate much more interesting. I had a girlfriend once who told me that I wasn't Mr. Right, I'm Mr. *Always* Right. Not good. Sometimes my being wrong ignites a TV program because it takes the presentation in unexpected directions. Nobody's right all the time. So when the facts overwhelm you, admit it.

Rule Five: Don't be a phony, be genuine on the air. Now, this rule presents problems for some TV newspeople because they are nasty people in real life, and misanthropy rarely works out for a TV anchor. Years ago, the late Charles Kuralt was an unpleasant guy to me and other young CBS News reporters, but the public thought he was a great guy. Kuralt was a total phony on the air and made millions doing it. But his airtime was limited. His tightly edited reports were only a few minutes long and were sometimes spaced a week apart.

If you're on the air every day and are disingenuous, the folks will most likely pick it up. There are exceptions, though. Walter Cronkite was a difficult person, but he still came across as a trusted on-air uncle each night.

Having worked in the business for a while, I was tired of TV charlatans and resolved to be my real self on the air for better or for worse. With my personality, that was an enormous risk, but one many of you clearly appreciated.

THE POWER OF BLUNT COMMENTARY

My Fox News colleagues tell me that folks often ask them, "What is O'Reilly *really* like?" The underlying question is, of course: Is he a Pinhead or what?

Well, to help answer that question, I must admit that some people have considered me a Pinhead since my earliest days in the bassinet. I was definitely considered a Pinhead in some precincts of Chaminade High School on Long Island, and the same was true in college. As an illustration, please allow me to share my first major journalistic controversy with you because, as we know, sharing is the mark of a Patriot.

The year was 1971. The Vietnam War controversy was raging all across the country. It was the hottest issue on nearly every American college campus. The school I was attending, Marist College, located in the garden spot of Poughkeepsie, New York, was basically a working-class place gone wild. When I first showed up as a freshman in the fall of 1967, an excessive quantity of beer was the mind-altering substance of choice. But in the winter of '71, drugs had flooded the campus, and then it became "power to the people" time.

I didn't buy it.

I had returned to Marist as a senior after spending my junior year abroad at the University of London. There I saw the antiwar movement trash Berkeley Square (home of the American embassy) and basically cause unnecessary mayhem and destruction in the name of "peace."

I was skeptical of the antiwar zealots because most of the guys I knew who were involved with intense protest were hopheads, stoners, unwashed zombies. Remember, I was a football, baseball, and ice hockey player. My comfort zone was sporting activity, not bongs and acid.

But I wasn't a moron. I knew some of the Levittown guys who had been drafted and sent to Vietnam. When they came back home, many of them were very different people, affected with a myriad of emotional problems. And they all said the same thing: it was brutally chaotic over there.

Disturbed by the condition of my neighborhood pals, I listened closely to both sides of the Vietnam debate and tried to educate myself as to what was really going on. Did America want to kill babies on purpose, as the Yippie Abbie Hoffman was screaming? Was the United States the second coming of the Third Reich? I had a hard time accepting the SDS (Students for a Democratic Society) chant: "Hey, hey, LBJ, how many kids did you kill today?"

Not that I had any use for President Lyndon Johnson. I didn't. But my country was under assault from all directions, and my instinct was that much of it was unfair. History, I believe, has proved me right. After the United States left Southeast Asia, far worse things occurred than had during the war. The rampaging Communists murdered millions of innocent people. Years later, I assigned *Factor* producer Jesse Watters to confront Jane Fonda, a major Pinhead and communist sympathizer, with the actions of the Khmer Rouge and the North Vietnamese. Typically, Ms. Fonda said that the Killing Fields of Cambodia never would have happened had America not started all the trouble in the first place. No way Jane was gonna assign any moral blame to her guys. She'll go to her grave blaming America for just about everything. If you are still in doubt about what a Pinhead really is, take Jane out to dinner.

So despite all the trouble in 1971, I still believed the USA was a noble nation, but there was no doubt in my mind that things were screwed up in Southeast Asia.

That was my point of view at age twenty-one as I sat in Dr. Carolyn Landau's political science class. But the professor was not nearly as conflicted as I was about America. No, she *knew* we were an evil empire and was not shy in listing the grave sins our nation was committing, not only in Vietnam but also back home. Her class was one long anti-American screed. But I had to sit through it because I needed the credits to graduate.

Dr. Landau, since departed, loathed your humble correspondent, perhaps because I showered daily, unlike some refugees from Woodstock. Certainly, she thought I was a Pinhead and awarded me a C in the class, my lowest collegiate grade. I'm not a whiner, so I swallowed the C. But then a funny thing happened on my way to Pinhead-or-Patriot status. I struck up a conversation with a classmate—a guy named Trent who had cut 90 percent of Landau's lectures. In fact, Trent showed up for just three poli-sci classes the entire semester. Somehow he was MIA for the other seventeen. Despite that, the guy was awarded an A by Landau. Did I mention that Trent was African American?

"You got an A?" I said to him.

"Right on."

"But you never showed up."

"Don't have to show up with Landau. Just have to be a brother."

"What?"

"Everyone knows she has a thing for us."

Trent then laughed and walked away.

That did it. I immediately put pen to paper. I had an outlet because I'd been writing a column for the student newspaper, the

Circle, for three years. And so, on January 21, 1971, the no-spin zone officially began with the following article, which I am reprising the way it was originally written, bad grammar and all:

ATTITUDES: OUTRAGEOUS
By Bill O'Reilly

Good morning, class, welcome to Political Science 203. My name is Dr. Landleft and all I have to say is, "Power to the people."

This semester's work will be very interesting providing you have the right attitude. I know there is some talk around campus to the effect that I do not give an objective course. This talk was obviously started by some disturbed fascists and it definitely has racist overtones, as I'm sure you can all see.

Well, to dispel all of my critics, I have decided to assign readings concerning both the Left and the Right. The first two books, which will be read by tomorrow, are the "Agony of the New Left," by Fidel Castro and "Danger on the Right," by Gore Vidal.

Hey, I just thought of a joke. If Fidel Castro married Gore Vidal he'd be—Fidel Vidal!

I just noticed that a few of the slower ones in the class did not laugh at that joke. Well, I have your names, you can be sure of that. Don't misunderstand me, you are under no obligation to laugh at my jokes or say yes to everything I say. You are all free to dissent—no matter how misguided and immature that dissent may be. I like people to dissent. As you know, I'm a revolutionary myself. But keep in mind who has the power here.

"The people, right, Dr. Landleft?"

Er, yes. Who said that? Oh, the black lad, very good,

very good. I bet you had a hard time growing up in the ghetto with the FBI always hounding your parents?

"Not really, Doctor. My father is a detective."

Oh, well, you can be sure you'll be treated equally in this class. In fact, you get an A.

Well, class, let's get back to the subject. What is it again? Oh, yes, Political Science. As you all know, Spiro and the CIA are all around us and closing in fast. Perhaps we might have to take to the streets.

"Dr. Landleft, I have a question."

Oh, my God. Well, go ahead.

"Why is it that communistic regimes always wind up as repressive states?"

"That question is not relevant, it's the kind of question that only a neo-Nazi would ask. Besides, it's off-topic and we must always stay on-topic."

"Dr. Landleft, I think that question pertains to Political Science."

"I decide what pertains to the subject around here. My class is liberal but I must have some control, right? Of course, I'm right. Let me throw this out for discussion: We all know that here in racist Amerika, notice that I spell the country with a K instead of a C. Isn't that right on? Anyway, what do you think can be done to overthrow the present government? Yes, that student."

"I don't think we ought to overthrow the government, Dr. Landleft."

"Wrong! Someone else? Yes, the longhaired student wearing that 'put the pigs in the pen' button."

"Uh, I really didn't hear your question, I wasn't listening."

"Exactly. The whole class could take a lesson from that student."

ATTITUDES: OUTRAGEOUS
by BILL O'REILLY

Good morning class welcome to Political Science 203. My name is Mrs. Landleft and all I have to say is, "Power to the People."

This semester's work will be very interesting provided you have the right attitude. I know there is some talk around campus to the effect that I do not give an objective course. This talk was obviously started by some disturbed fascists and it definitely has racist overtones as I'm sure you all can see.

Well, to dispel all of my critics I have decided to assign readings concerning both the left and the ridiculous right. The first two books, which will be read by tomorrow, are the "Agony of the New Left" by Fidel Castro and "The Danger on the Right" by Gore Vidal. Right class? Of course I'm right.

Hey, I just thought of a joke. This will liven things up. If Fidel Castro married Gore Vidal he'd be - Fidel Vidal. Fairly humorous, right class? Of course I'm right.

I just noticed that a few of the slower ones in the class did not laugh at that joke. Well, I have your names, you can be sure of that. Don't misunderstand me, you are under no obligation to laugh at my jokes or say yes to everything I say. You are all free to dissent - no matter how immature and misguided that dissent may be. I like people to dissent, as you know I'm a revolutionary myself. But keep in mind who has the power here. The people, right, Mrs. Landleft.

Er, yes, who said that? Oh, the black lad, very good, very good. I bet you had a hard time growing up in the ghetto with the F.B.I. always hounding your parents?

Not really Mrs. Landleft, you see I grew up in Hyde Park and my father is a detective.

Oh, well you can be sure you'll be treated equally in this class. In fact you get an A.

Well class, let's get back to the subject. What is it again - oh yeah, Political Science. As you all know Spiro and the C.I.A. are all around us and closing in fast. Perhaps we should take to the jungle like Regis Debray. That's an idea! The next class will be held behind Sheahan Hall in the forest. Everyone wear old army jackets and berets and we'll run around and practice guerrilla tactics. We might even capture the new parking lot and blow up Bro. Donelly's tractor.

Mrs. Landleft, Mrs. Landleft. What, What!

Isn't this supposed to be a Political Science course?

Yes.

Well, I have a question concerning Political Science.

Oh my God. Well, go ahead.

Why is it that all Communistic regimes always wind up as repressive states?

That question is not relevant, it is the kind of question that only a neo-nazi would ask. And besides it's off the topic and we must always stay on the topic.

Mrs. Landleft, I think that that question pertains to the topic.

Foolish Boy, I decide what pertains to the topic around here. My class is liberal but I must have some control, right? Of course I'm right. Let me throw this out for discussion. We all know that here in RACIST

CON'T. P. 4 - Col. 5

Circle this news story! Here's my first brush with political commentary.

Well, my first venture into the world of contentious journalism was not exactly like the sharp-witted work of Pulitzer Prize–winning journalist Mike Royko, but it sure did stir things up at Marist College and, unbeknownst to me at the time, launched my flamboyant career. Letters poured in to the *Circle*, and they were pretty much evenly divided over whether I was a Pinhead or Patriot. You know, it's kind of eerie. What happened almost forty years ago is precisely what's happening to me today. I learned the power of blunt commentary and reacted with bemusement as long as the criticism wasn't personal. I didn't know it at the time, but that rudimentary column about the nutty professor was the beginning of a beautiful friendship between me, opinionated journalism, and millions of Americans.

Back then (as now), I didn't worry too much about those who called me a Pinhead (mostly behind my back, since I am six-four). I liked the action that controversy brought, and I was able to whack Dr. Landau, who certainly deserved it.

To this day, millions of people think that I am just awful because I say things they don't like. For example, the actor George Clooney certainly thinks I'm a Pinhead. Back in 2001, I suggested that he and other Hollywood stars track the money they raised for the families of those killed on 9/11. You may remember that Clooney didn't like some punk (me) demanding accountability from him and his swell friends, so he ran around taking my name in vain. I was much amused, and the controversy brought great ratings, a very important thing for any media Patriot, or Pinhead for that matter.

After thinking about the situation for a while, I replied to Clooney's angst with my usual eloquence. I called *him* a Pinhead. Let the playground rank-out session begin.

Thank God (and I do), millions of other folks respect the fact that I speak my mind bluntly and honestly. After all, isn't that what a Patriot does? Or am I wrong?

CHAPTER 8

Loathing Obama

He's a SOCIALIST!
—*The Greek Chorus*

IF YOU HATE any American President, you are a Pinhead. I simply cannot understand why people do that. Bill Clinton, George W. Bush, Barack Obama—all these guys were and are loathed by millions of their fellow citizens. Here's my question: WHY WASTE YOUR TIME?

Hatred is *the* most powerful emotion, one that can lead to violence. It is far more intense than love and, left unchecked, can actually destroy the one who hates. If you can possibly avoid hating, please do that.

But I am not Yoko Ono. I well understand evil, betrayal, and destruction. I've seen all of those things up close and personal. And do you know what? I've come to hate some of the evildoers. I seriously despise them and do whatever I legally and morally can to neutralize their activities. This genuine loathing for the merchants of destruction motivates me to take them on. So I'm able to use this kind of "hatred" in a positive way. Or so I tell myself.

But hating Barack Obama or George W. Bush is a neurosis. These men do not deserve that. You can disagree with them all day long and vocalize your disenchantment to all who will listen. But really, hating these guys is something that you should think about, because it could harm you.

That being said, you may sincerely believe that your place in the age of Obama is not a good place. And if that's the case, you have the right to dislike the President's belief system and actions very, very much. Certainly, the President is trying to change the country by imposing his version of "social justice." In this effort, some Americans will be helped and some will be harmed. If you are being harmed, it is only natural for you to frown on Mr. Obama. But there's a long way between dislike and hate.

As we discussed earlier in the Rush Limbaugh–Bill O'Reilly pages, some Americans sincerely believe that Barack Obama is a socialist who is trying to alter our free-market way of life. If you love the free market, as I do, you may hate that perceived action. That's logical. But you should not hate the man. That's irrational.

BELOW-AVERAGE MARX ON THE SOCIALISM TEST

Is the President truly a socialist? Not if you define socialism as government *ownership* of business and private property. Yes, the Obama administration is interfering in the marketplace by upping government oversight of the financial industry, as well as bailing out some car companies and banks with taxpayer money. But past administrations have also done this kind of stuff in times of economic emergency. Therefore, opining that Mr. Obama is on a par with, say, Karl Marx, is foolish. There's a huge difference between the President and hard-core socialists who will seize your hat at the drop of it.

But my pal Glenn Beck and some of my viewers observe it differently, believing that I am an incredible Pinhead for denying what they see as obvious. If it walks like a duck, they say. Okay, I get that Van Jones and Assistant Secretary of State Michael Posner are Far Left guys. I get that the President did not object to the fiery anti-American nonsense of the Reverend Wright and the radical résumé of Bill Ayers. There is no question that Barack Obama does not see the fringe left as all that objectionable. That's what can happen when you attend Harvard and work on the south side of Chicago. But, as I wrote in my newspaper column, socialism is defined as a system in which the means of producing and distributing goods is owned collectively.

Yes, President Obama has intruded into the private sector in the areas of health and finance. As I mentioned, he also wants big-time federal oversight on the financial and energy industries. All of that is true. But I have produced this book, and Obama can't intrude on that. He'll tax the hell out of my profits, but these pages are not a "collective" effort. They belong to my publisher, HarperCollins, and to me.

Until Barack Obama begins to insinuate himself into the livelihoods of American workers, he cannot accurately be described as a socialist. A quasi-socialist, maybe. A Pinhead about economic matters, probably.

Nevertheless, my mailbag is on fire. Kathy from Georgia wrote: "Bill, why does the question of whether Obama is a socialist bother you so? Let me verify it. Yes, he's a socialist. Does that make you feel better?"

Not really, Kathy.

John, who lives in Louisiana, opined: "O'Reilly, so you don't think Obama is a socialist? Duh!"

Indeed.

Obviously, anti-Obama passions are currently running high in America, but here's an interesting observation: the Obama angst almost exactly mirrors the anti-Bush madness. Different folks, same strokes. He (fill in Bush or Obama) is the devil. He's a joke. He's ruining the country! In both cases, I feel criticism was overdone.

As I wrote this book, I was feeling fairly confident about my Obama analysis and believed I was putting forth a fair and balanced portrait of the President. Then, speaking in Illinois about Wall Street reform on April 28, 2010, Mr. Obama said this:

> *We're not trying to push financial reform because we begrudge success that's fairly earned. I mean, I do think at a certain point you've made enough money. But part of the American way is you can just keep on making it if you're providing a good product or providing a good service.*

You've made enough money? Oy.

See, once a President or other powerful politician starts telling folks they've made enough money, all hell breaks loose. The American dream is unlimited. If you want to be a billionaire, you can try. If you want to teach school for $80,000 a year, you can do that, too. It should be all up to you, not to President Obama.

When he says stuff like that, the socialism flags come out. And that's not irrational. Again, if it walks like a duck.

Let me make one more attempt here to define what I think Barack Obama believes about currency and social justice. Based upon my time at Harvard and working with hundreds of liberals in the media industry, I see the President as a man committed to leveling the playing field. That means he is down with taking as much money as he can from affluent Americans, and giving said cash to those who do not have much. The President is a big income-redistribution guy. He's a big social justice guy. He sincerely believes that federal power should be expanded to make life better for the have-nots by instituting a series of expensive government-funded entitlements. Therefore, he walks a tightrope. Wages and investment income are, after all, a form of private property. You earned it, it's yours. But Barack Obama wants at least some of yours, and the Constitution gives Congress the right to tax us. So the question becomes, just how far will Mr. Obama eventually go to impose his view of social justice on the country? Already, ObamaCare is the biggest entitlement since the New Deal, and federal spending is at record levels. So to be fair, I can't call Americans who believe Obama is a full-blown socialist Pinheads. Under his cool demeanor, he might have a big "S" on his chest just as Superman does. But I think not. As I've said before and will again, I think he is the most liberal President ever elected in this country, but he is not a stealth Hugo Chavez.

As always, I could be wrong.

CHAPTER 9

★

All-Time Favorite P&Ps

THIS IS MY FAVORITE CHAPTER in this book. I will be completely irresponsible in the upcoming pages, and by the way, there is no pattern to what's contained in them. It's stream of consciousness time. I will discuss dozens of famous and semi-famous people, assigning them Pinhead or Patriot status. Defying the ancient TV program *Dragnet*, no names will be changed to protect the innocent or guilty, as the case may be.

Of course, this entire chapter is grossly unfair. My evaluations are completely subjective. Yes, I will use facts to back up my assertions, as I always do. But these facts have been selected to bolster my ultimate judgment on the individuals in question. I mean, I could have picked *anyone* for this chapter, but these names *just came to me*. In other words, I am not playing devil's advocate here. I am designating blame and praise based upon my personal whim. I did not poll these people, or ask the opinions of others. Blame me for this entire fiasco.

Let's begin with a few Presidents. As you may have heard, I own an extensive research trove of primary source material concerning the nation's chief executives. That means I possess some of their letters, manuscripts, and other personal items. It's a fabulous hobby, and I have learned a tremendous amount by reading the personal thoughts and correspondence of these men, most of whom, but not all, were Patriots.

Recently, Siena College, located in upstate New York, polled a group of historians about the best and worst Presidents. Franklin D. Roosevelt came out on top; Teddy Roosevelt was ranked second, followed by Abraham Lincoln, George Washington, and Thomas Jefferson. Andrew Johnson, the only President impeached aside from Bill Clinton, came in dead last. George W. Bush came in 39th out of 44 while Barack Obama was ranked 15th.

The Obama positioning tells you all you need to know about this poll. It's nonsense. President Obama is having major trouble, and outside of passing an unpopular health care law, our current leader has achieved little—even counting his Nobel Peace Prize. Nevertheless, he's number 15! Come on. By any fair measure, this is stupid. Actually, it was unfair even to include Mr. Obama in the poll. Let the man at least finish his first term before evaluating him.

So we know the poll skews Left; that's why FDR and Obama did well. In this book, however, we don't skew any way but fairly, so let's take a look at some Presidents to see which have been Pinheads and which have been Patriots.

ABRAHAM LINCOLN

Hands down, the best President ever. Compared to what he faced with Southern states seceding all over the place, most other

Presidents' terms were like Caribbean vacations. Only Franklin Delano Roosevelt, who had to deal with the Great Depression and then World War II, faced anything comparable to old Abe.

And speaking of depression, Lincoln was afflicted with sometimes crippling "melancholia," which is what they called acute depression back then. Plagued with frequent bouts of gloom and despair, he fought through them even while under incredible stress.

Remember, the South was winning the Civil War right up until the battle of Gettysburg. Lincoln knew that hundreds of thousands of Americans were being killed and maimed in brutal warfare. Because of his determination to save the Union, he never wavered. His young son died, his wife was often unstable, and his generals let him down time after time. Yet Lincoln soldiered on and literally kept the United States from fracturing by employing sheer force of will. A great lesson for all Americans—never fold, fight to the end.

Abraham Lincoln was compassionate, brave, and unselfish, and he loved his country intensely. There is no better example of a true Patriot than the man from Hodgen's Mill, Kentucky.

GEORGE WASHINGTON

Ranking just a notch below Lincoln on the presidential chart, Washington was amazingly brave and always put his country before his own self-glorification.

For eight years, Washington fought a guerilla-like campaign against the powerful British army and navy. He had little going for him since supplies were scant and his forces were constantly on the run. But the man remained steadfast; he alone inspired the colonial forces to stick it out despite their intense physical sufferings. At his Valley Forge winter headquarters, Washington lost a quarter of his men to disease in a matter of months.

George Washington, the man, was a quiet guy, a bit distant, with few close friends. But his troops and, later, his presidential cabinet loved him—primarily because of his basic decency. So how do I know that? Well, that's an excellent question. Most history books glamorize men like Washington and Lincoln, making it very hard to get a true read on them, no pun intended. But, as I mentioned, I have some excellent primary source historical material in my possession and one letter proves my contention about Washington.

Written shortly after the Battle of Bunker (Breed's) Hill by General Horatio Gates, Washington's second-in-command, the letter orders Colonel Artemus Ward and other colonial officers not to abuse captured British prisoners. Gates wrote this on August 1, 1775:

> *His Excellency General Washington is very desirous that you give very particular directions to the principal surgeons in your department to take the greatest care of the poor unhappy [British] Marines who were wounded in the late attack upon the lighthouse; if no other good consequence should arise from a particular tenderness and attention to them at this time, we have our reward in the consciousness of doing and performing that humanity to conquered enemies, which, it is a shameful reproach and an everlasting stigma to General Gage, he has not shown to the poor and distressed inhabitants of Boston.*

This is an extraordinary piece of history that clearly demonstrates a vital fact: the father of our country was a humane man even in the face of intense provocation. As the Gates letter tells us, the British "Redcoats" under the command of Thomas Gage were brutal to the people who lived in and around Boston. Yet Washington went out of his way to establish strict humanitarian rules for those captured by his forces. At the time, that kind of order was extremely rare because feelings of revenge were running high on both sides.

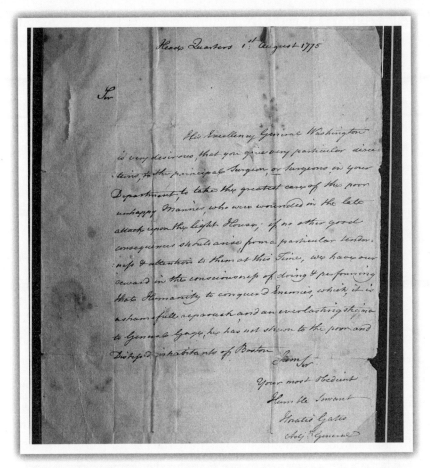

The nation's first President was one of the original human rights activists, as this missive from General Gates on Washington's behalf indicates.

By his perspicacity, George Washington established the U.S. government as an entity that seeks justice and extends mercy. His actions defined the newly formed United States as a noble nation. His brilliant performance during the Revolutionary War and subsequent leadership as President set an example that all American politicians should seek to emulate. Too bad many of them don't.

My admiration for George Washington is total. He is the gold standard as far as Patriotism is concerned.

ANDREW JACKSON

Quick quiz question: What does Old Hickory have in common with Barack Obama? Well, both he and Obama won presidential elections with more than 50 percent of the vote. Only four Democrats in history have done that, Lyndon Johnson and FDR being the other two. But that is where the Jackson comparisons with our current President end.

Andrew Jackson was a guy who essentially hated Washington, both the town and the federal government. He thought the political establishment was rife with crooks, and he was correct, although, perhaps hypocritically, as he himself rewarded all kinds of cronies upon being elected.

Of this I'm sure: if he were alive today, ol' Andy would be horrified by Mr. Obama's expansion of the federal apparatus and would trust none of it. A 13-trillion-dollar deficit? Jackson would call out the militia.

Andrew Jackson was a brutal guy. As a boy in South Carolina, he watched the British commit atrocities during the Revolutionary War. Young Andy himself was scarred after being beaten by an English soldier. But then as a man, he turned around and committed horrifying war crimes himself. To this day, some Native Americans, especially those from the Cherokee tribe, refuse to carry $20 bills because they don't want to see Jackson's face. Indians well remember what Jackson did to the tribes living in the Southeast. For example, he forced the largely peaceful Cherokee Nation off their land, marching them west of the Mississippi River in the infamous Trail of Tears atrocity. It is estimated that more than four thousand Cherokees perished during that ordeal, many of them women, children, and elderly. There is no excuse for such treatment. Brutality is brutality whether it is 1830 or 2010.

Many working-class white folks, however, loved Jackson. To them, he was the man who both hammered the British at the Battle of New

Orleans and proved his mettle as a courageous Indian fighter. Once he got to Washington, Jackson attacked corruption in the banking industry and dealt harshly with the states' rights issues that threatened to divide the country. It is quite likely that some Southern states would have seceded from the Union during Jackson's presidency had he not been such a tough guy. In fact, I have a letter written by Harry Truman assessing Jackson and President James Buchanan:

> *History will tell you, however, that old Buch was short on decision, and had he acted with the firmness of Andrew Jackson, for instance, in his dealing with the problems of the South, the War Between the States might well have been averted.*

Nevertheless, human lives trump policy, so Andrew Jackson has to be held responsible for his brutal nature. Unlike Washington and Lincoln, who were inherently merciful, Jackson was hard-hearted. On balance, he did some good things for the nation, but overall, I have to designate him a Pinhead.

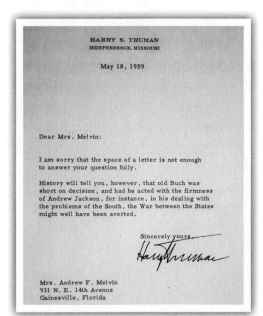

You gotta love it. In this letter from my personal collection, Harry Truman is stopping just short of calling James Buchanan a Pinhead (probably because I hadn't popularized the word yet!).

TEDDY ROOSEVELT

Here is the original no-spin guy. Want straight talk? T. R. is your man. After William McKinley was assassinated in September 1901, Roosevelt became President at age forty-three, the youngest man ever to sit in the White House. He probably said to himself *What took so long?*

Loud, fast-talking, and sometimes manic, T. R. drove some of his assistants crazy; more than a few even fled the room. He himself had no room for BS. I have a letter written by him in which he absolutely lays out President Woodrow Wilson:

> *Wilson is in no sense of the word an idealist, but he is a doctrinaire. We probably have never had a President so devoid of regard for real ethics, based on conduct and deeds.*

THE KANSAS CITY STAR

OFFICE OF
THEODORE ROOSEVELT

NEW YORK OFFICE
147 MADISON AVEN

December 31st, 1918.

My dear Dr. Bogert:

I thank you for sending me the article. I doubt, however, if I should care to enter into a controversy with a gentleman of whom I have never heard. Mr. Lynch has deliberately mis-stated the facts, and when a man deliberately mis-states facts there is little use of entering a controversy with him. I said that not one American in a thousand knew of Mr. Wilson's Fourteen Points. Mr. Lynch cannot deny this, and so he deliberately falsifies the truth and says that I deny that the American people knew that this was a war for world justice and righteousness and for world democracy! I wish to repeat that when Mr. Lynch makes this statement he deliberately and wilfully falsifies the truth. He knows I never said any such thing. Again Mr. Lynch falsifies the truth when he says that I advocate huge armaments. Mr. Wilson has advocated that the American nation have a navy the size of Great Britain's, and go into a rivalry with Great Britain in the matter of building a navy. I have repudiated this attempt to make us build a huge "spite" navy. I have said that this nation should have a system of universal training substantially like the Swiss. No man, who isn't a fool

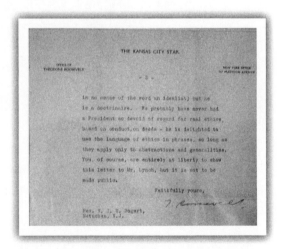

THE KANSAS CITY STAR

OFFICE OF
THEODORE ROOSEVELT
— 2 —

NEW YORK OFFICE
1ST MADISON AVENUE

huge military armament. For once he is correct
when he says that I believe in nationalism;
but he deliberately fails to state that I have
pointed out that sound nationalism is the only
basis for international co-operation and unity.

Mr. Lynch doubtless neither desires
to tell the truth nor is he capable of doing so.
If he did he would remember and would state that
it was I who for two and a half years stood for
international justice on behalf of Belgium and
against the foul iniquities of Germany, when
Mr. Wilson with every species of misrepresentation
was deluding the American people, was putting peace
above righteousness, and was actually, in his
Presidential Address of 1915, going to the length
of saying that he abhored and condemned Americans
who upheld the cause of Belgium and the allies as
against Germany, and regarded these men as worse
than the German murderers and dynamiters. As a
clergyman recently remarked to me, in all these
two and a half years there isn't a trace of
recognition of any real principle of ethics in
anything Mr. Wilson has said, having reference to
any concrete case of wrong doing. Mr. Wilson is

THE KANSAS CITY STAR

OFFICE OF
THEODORE ROOSEVELT
— 3 —

NEW YORK OFFICE
1ST MADISON AVENUE

in no sense of the word an idealist; but he
is a doctrinaire. We probably have never had
a President so devoid of regard for real ethics,
based on conduct, on deeds — he is delighted to
use the language of ethics in phrases, so long as
they apply only to abstractions and generalities.
You, of course, are entirely at liberty to show
this letter to Mr. Lynch, but it is not to be
made public.

Faithfully yours,

T. Roosevelt

Rev. T. J. H. Bogert,
Metuchen, N.J.

Here Teddy Roosevelt speaks his mind about Woodrow Wilson. He would have
made a great guest on the *Factor* if he were alive today, addressing everything
from Wall Street to the environment like he did back in the day!

Roosevelt thought Wilson was a weak-willed academic who lacked the *cojones* to control the world's bad guys, something Roosevelt relished doing perhaps too much. For example, the Rough Rider deal was overplayed. To say the Spanish opposition in Cuba was hapless is to insult haps everywhere.

But Teddy R. did a number of very impressive things, two of which have stood the test of time. First, he took on big corporations who were subverting capitalism by ruthlessly imposing monopolies on a largely unsophisticated public. Roosevelt busted some of the so-called trusts, and did it with efficiency and determination. Like Andrew Jackson, if Teddy were alive today, he would bitterly oppose government bailouts of fat-cat companies and Wall Street corruption in general.

Second, Teddy was green, setting aside millions of acres of land for public use. His environmental policies, particularly in the West, are still benefiting the nation today. Ironically, T. R. was an avid game hunter. Perhaps he protected nature to benefit himself. But he did protect the land and loved nature in its pristine state.

On balance, I say, "bully!" Certainly, Teddy Roosevelt was not the second-best President of all time, but he was definitely a Patriot and you gotta love him!

U. S. GRANT

Whenever I travel to Washington, I try to stay at the Willard Hotel near the White House. It was here that Abraham Lincoln lived before his inauguration, and it was in this hotel that the term *lobbyist* was first coined.

Here's the story: most days after a tough time in the White House, President U. S. Grant would repair to the Willard Hotel for a few cocktails to, um, unwind. Knowing this, folks wanting favors from Grant would wait in the hotel's lobby, adjacent to the bar.

When old Ulysses eventually wobbled out of said bar, these favor seekers would walk up and petition him, knowing that he would be a bit mellower after a few libations. Thus, the word *lobbyist* came into usage.

There is no question that U. S. Grant liked his booze, or that his drinking cost him dearly. His administration was full of crooks, including his own brother, but Grant, as most historians submit, had no idea of the graft going on around him. Ironically, he was able to cut through the fog of war to defeat Robert E. Lee and the Confederate forces, but he never did cut through the fog of inebriation to deal effectively with government corruption as President.

So regretfully, U. S. Grant is a hybrid: a Patriot as a general, a Pinhead as a President.

JAMES BUCHANAN

Old Buch was hands down the worst President of all time, with apologies to the aforementioned Andrew Johnson as well as Franklin Pierce, both of whom tried hard for the title. Buchanan did absolutely nothing during his four years in office. As the country was aflame with controversy over slavery and the intense states' rights debate, Buchanan upheld the legality of slavery, while at the same time saying he was personally opposed to it. To confuse matters more, he also opposed the abolitionist movement, calling its members extremists. Since nobody ever knew what this guy was talking about, South Carolina basically told him to go f— himself. Buchanan then sent a federal warship to scare South Carolina out of seceding from the Union, but as soon as the ship was fired upon it hastily left the harbor.

Buchanan's response to an attack on a federal warship was to do nothing. From the time he was elected in 1856 to the time he was booted out in favor of Abraham Lincoln in 1860, James Buchanan slept in the White House but did little else. Barney Fife could have done a better job.

Buchanan's most famous quote as President was to Mr. Lincoln: "My dear, sir, if you are as happy on entering the White House as I on leaving, you are a very happy man indeed."

To which I hope Lincoln replied, "Hey, Jim, don't let the door hit you in the . . . Pinhead."

DWIGHT EISENHOWER

My parents loved this guy. As a little boy in 1956, I remember my mother singing his presidential campaign song:

> *I like Ike.*
> *I'll say it again and again.*
> *I like Ike.*
> *Let him finish the job he began!*

I thought the song was kind of dopey, not nearly as catchy as the Davy Crockett song I sang all day long. But my parent's appreciation for the man is understandable.

General Eisenhower emerged as America's top hero after World War II; he fully deserved the label. Keeping the Allied Forces in Europe united and fighting hard was no easy task when you had eccentrics like Charles de Gaulle, Winston Churchill, and General Bernard Law Montgomery in your face. But Eisenhower held it together and, like Washington and Lincoln, did not exact revenge on the enemy, even though that enemy, Nazi Germany, was among the most savage in history.

As President, Eisenhower was cautious and kind of dull, perfectly reflecting the decade he dominated, the 1950s. After the Great

Depression, World War II, and the Korean War, Americans needed a break. Ike gave it to them. Hot dogs, baseball, and apple pie. *Father Knows Best,* and so did Ed Sullivan, Lawrence Welk, Perry Como, and Frank Sinatra. One of the few disruptions to the placid culture was Elvis. But even the "Hound Dog" guy was polite and nice to his mother.

There is something to be said for a calming influence, especially after terrible turmoil. Eisenhower provided that. But privately, the man had a temper and held strong opinions.

Here I can reveal for the first time publically that the general was not a big fan of the Kennedy family. In 1968 he wrote a letter to his close friend General Robert Cutler in which he excoriated Robert Kennedy, who was campaigning for the Democratic presidential nomination:

> *Two or three things are bothering me very much about the political situation these days. First, I am disgusted at the newspaper accounts of Kennedy's receptions throughout the country, at least in Kansas and California. It is difficult for me to see a single qualification that the man has for the presidency. I think he is shallow, vain, and untrustworthy—on top of which he is indecisive. Yet, his attraction for so many people is extraordinary. In my opinion what he would do to this country, if elected, would be nothing at all to what has happened to it over these past seven years!*

While everyone "liked Ike," clearly Ike didn't like everyone in return. What was it about RFK that made him write these harsh words?

GETTYSBURG
PENNSYLVANIA 17325
Indio, California
March 26, 1968

PERSONAL

Dear Bobby:

First of all, I am more than delighted to hear from you and even more delighted to know that you are at last determined to "slow up" and take care of yourself. The one thing that amazed me in your letter was your report from Governor Volpe that Dick Nixon thought I was vague in my memory of him and of his accomplishments. Something has gone completely haywire--not only do I remember Volpe distinctly, he is one of the men in political life for whom I have a great admiration.

I do recall that in my conversation with Dick, some speculation came as to a possible running mate for him, in the event that Dick should be nominated. While I do not remember the details of the conversation, I think the only question mark that was even hinted at concerning Volpe was the consideration of geography. I think it was suggested that if Dick were nominated from New York, there might be some thought in certain quarters that the other nominee should be from the Midwest or far West. This is the only possible explanation I can give for Dick's feeling that I was somewhat vague in my reactions to the Governor.

I am back in my office for the first time in more than a week, having been laid low by a sudden attack of the flu. It has been several days now since I have had a temperature, so yesterday morning my doctors let me try out my wings for a couple of hours.

I am amazed at the amount of money that you are able to collect for worthy causes in Boston; nevertheless, I think you have done your share and it is time to let someone else take over.

If you see Sinny, please do give him my warmest regard. I like him and I like to talk to him. I hope that I might get to see him again this coming summer.

Two or three things are bothering me very much about the political situation these days. First, I am disgusted at the newspaper accounts of Kennedy's receptions throughout the country, at least in Kansas and California. It is difficult for me to see a single qualification that the man has for the Presidency. I think he is shallow, vain and untrustworthy--on top of which, he is indecisive. Yet, his attraction for so many people is extraordinary. In my opinion, what he would do to this country, if elected, would be nothing at all to what has happened to it over these past seven years!

Another thing that puzzles me is the labels that the writers--and finally the public--pin upon various candidates according to the supposed nature of their political beliefs. For example, we now find Dick Nixon constantly referred to as a conservative or a rightist; certainly in our eight years I knew him as a "moderate" or what you might call a "middle-of-the-roader." Now the word moderate is applied to such individuals as Lindsay, Case, Javitts and others, including Rockefeller. Yet, in domestic affairs, I have been able to make very little differences in the political differences in the philosophies of Rockefeller and Nixon. Enough of this.

Mamie joins me in affectionate regard and very best wishes.

Devotedly,

[signature]

Brig. Gen. Robert Cutler
41 Beacon Street
Boston, Massachusetts 02108

Eisenhower, of course, was referring to the Vietnam debacle and the shocking cultural changes brought about by the Woodstock generation. As with many people his age, the old general must have been reeling as he watched the images of protest and social change on the nightly news. Somehow I can't picture him smoking weed and saying "far out."

I will deal with Robert Kennedy shortly and believe Ike's assessment of him is misguided, to say the least. But, for his time, Dwight Eisenhower was the right man for the presidency, as far as most Americans were concerned. He was a Patriot.

JIMMY CARTER

I lost faith in the man from Plains, Georgia, when I saw him and his wife, Rosalynn, sitting next to Michael Moore at the Democratic National Convention in 2004. The three were happily chatting away and seemed to be having a grand old time.

Now, I have nothing against Moore personally. He's an ideological nut who can be entertaining. But, please, a former President of the United States yukking it up in front of the nation with a guy who admires Fidel Castro? No. As my mom told me, you will be evaluated by the quality of your companions.

If Carter had the poor judgment to sit next to Far Right radio fanatic Michael Savage, I'd say the same thing.

Jimmy Carter tried hard in the Oval Office and has done some good charitable work throughout his life. No question about that. He is not a bad man. After the turmoil of the Nixon years, Carter, somewhat like Barack Obama, was seen as a refreshing outsider who might put the country back on track. That was 1976. Disco also exploded in 1976. You get the connection, I'm sure.

Anyway, Jimmy Carter got his small-town butt kicked in Washington. The economy was very bad, and even worse, Iran humiliated the United States by holding fifty-two Americans hostage for more than a year (prompting Walter Cronkite to remind the nation daily of exactly how many days the Americans had been held captive). Also, because of Carter's chaotic energy and foreign policies, there were enormous gas shortages throughout the United States. People waited on line for hours just to fill up their tanks. I was one of those people. It was awful.

Carter surrounded himself with cronies from Georgia and quickly was labeled a "rube" by the Washington establishment. I mean, it was bloody. When the Soviet Union invaded Afghanistan, Carter tried to scold them, but he looked weak doing so. On *Saturday Night Live*, Dan Aykroyd portrayed the President as a grinning bumpkin. After two years in office, the Carter presidency was in deep trouble. He came across as the mayor of Mayberry, not as an authoritative President.

After fighting off a brutal primary challenge by Ted Kennedy, Carter ran against Ronald Reagan in 1980 and lost big-time. In fact, Reagan never broke a sweat, swatting the beleaguered President in a debate by simply saying, "There you go again."

It is almost eerie that today we may be experiencing a giant flashback to the Carter era. President Obama's job approval rating is descending because of the economy, the oil spill, and overseas chaos, some of it generated by Iran. Will Obama be a Carter redux?

Jimmy Carter tried hard to be a Patriot; his service to America proves that. But he was also a terrible President, and that qualifies him as a Pinhead. So on balance, what's *your* verdict? I am betting you'll say Pinhead.

GERALD FORD

This man's life was also changed by the chaos Richard Nixon bequeathed the country. First, President Nixon appointed Ford, who was the Speaker of the House, to be vice President after the feds busted Spiro Agnew on a variety of corruption charges. By the way, "Ted" Agnew's dealings make Governor Rod Blagojevich look like a Patriot; he was that crooked.

Anyway, Gerald Ford was a decent guy who found himself in circumstances way beyond his control. Ten months after replacing Agnew, the man from Michigan was sworn in as President after Richard Nixon was forced to resign over the Watergate scandal. A month later, Ford pardoned Nixon, ending what he called "our long national nightmare." The pardon would come back to haunt him.

I had the opportunity to talk with Gerald Ford a number of times before he died in 2006. Among other things, he told me the presidential accomplishment of which he was most proud was the 1975 Helsinki Accord by which the Soviet Union renounced the use of military force to control countries in Eastern Europe like Poland and Hungary. Mr. Ford believed that this accord laid the groundwork for the eventual collapse of the Soviet Union almost twenty years later.

In 1976 Jimmy Carter easily defeated the incumbent Ford by fifty-seven electoral votes and close to two million popular votes. Ford lost the election largely because the media portrayed him as a bumbling fool. On *Saturday Night Live,* Chevy Chase played the President as a walking disaster, falling down every two minutes. Former President Lyndon Johnson described Ford, who was actually very athletic, as a man who had played too much football "without a helmet."

Gerald Ford had a chance to turn that perception around in the presidential debates with Carter, but he blew it. Ford came off as inarticulate and old next to the youthful, energetic governor of Georgia.

The truth is that Gerald Ford was a good man who was in over his head as President. Even though he was an establishment player, he devoted his life to his country. Thus, he goes into the Patriot category on his good intentions alone.

RONALD REAGAN

Now here's an interesting guy. Not as brilliant as his supporters purport, but very effective at leading the nation, especially in his second term when the pressure of reelection was off.

When Reagan left office in 1988, more Americans were working than at any other time in the nation's history. But in 1987, the stock market crashed more sharply than it had in 1929.

Reagan slashed taxes, but the national debt surpassed $1 trillion for the first time ever. By comparison, it is now $13 trillion, with bankruptcy a real possibility for the United States.

President Reagan spent freely on defense, a strategy that caused the Soviet Union to go bankrupt, or so some historians contend (correctly, I think). So on policy matters, President Reagan won some and lost some. His legacy, however, will be as a strong conservative leader.

Mr. Reagan was not a culture warrior per se. He did not relish confrontation the way CWs have to. But he was firm in his beliefs. I have a letter written in Reagan's hand to a proabortion advocate on Long Island:

> *I have a very deep belief that interrupting a pregnancy means the taking of a human life. In our Judeo-Christian tradition this can only be justified as a matter of self defense.*

That kind of clarity made Ronald Reagan an inspiring leader to many Americans. Even if you disagree with him, you would have to acknowledge that he brought prestige and authority to the White House, which was badly needed after President Carter's chaotic term. Even though the press constantly derided him, Reagan was able to communicate directly to the folks, frustrating the national media. ABC White House correspondent Sam Donaldson told me at the time that Reagan never made a decision unless "Mommy" signed off on it. "Mommy," of course, was Nancy Reagan. Donaldson and some other Washington reporters thought Reagan was an unsophisticated thinker, a rube who did not deserve to lead the country.

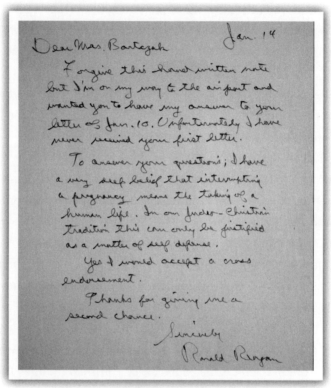

Ronald Reagan took a moment to handwrite this personal note to a proabortion advocate about his deep beliefs in opposition to abortion.

Finally, both President Reagan and President Obama have one significant thing in common: both saw their poll numbers dive in their second year in office. Reagan, as you all know, made a comeback that qualifies him for major Patriot status.

Mr. Obama has time left in office for the same to occur, but he also has a long climb back.

BUSH THE ELDER

Short takes: Like him. War hero. Entire career devoted to serving his country. Not good at reading lips. Told me the *New York Times* and Dan Rather treated him unfairly. Which is true. Mediocre President who got caught in the recession blues. As did his son W., which is kinda ironic. Benefited slightly from *Saturday Night Live* impressionist Dana Carvey's "wouldn't be prudent" line. Patriot.

WARREN HARDING

Only James Buchanan saves him from consideration as the worst President of all time. Harding was a good card player who took over the country in the wake of World War I. But he was ultimately disgraced. If you don't know what the Teapot Dome scandal was, trust me, it was not good. Neither was Harding, who did little in office other than play poker and spend taxpayer money on lavish dinner parties.

Word is, somebody may have poisoned Mr. Harding. He died in San Francisco's Palace Hotel at age fifty-eight. We cannot confirm the rumors of murder, but his wife did refuse an autopsy. He was in the city by the bay as part of his cross-country "Voyage of Understanding," a political ploy meant to showcase him talking with regular folks who told him, as we can now report, that he was a Pinhead.

NOW LET'S MOVE ON to some prominent Americans who have affected the country in both good and bad ways. Again, this is just a list I came up with. There is no reason or order to it. Some might say these musings are the product of a damaged mind. But, of course, folks who would opine that way are Pinheads.

ROBERT KENNEDY

Unlike Dwight Eisenhower's view of the man, I believe RFK was a great Patriot for two reasons: First, as attorney general under his brother the President, he aggressively took on organized crime when FBI director J. Edgar Hoover would not. And secondly, Kennedy spent an enormous amount of time disrupting the corrupt local and state police system in the South that was brutalizing African Americans during the civil rights era. Both actions make Kennedy not only a Patriot but a true American hero.

So how do I know what Kennedy did? Well, federal wiretaps from the early 1960s show top-ranking members of La Cosa Nostra ("our thing") venting their hatred for RFK. One thug is quoted as saying, "Bob Kennedy won't stop until he puts all of us in jail all over the country." When killers hate you—that's a good thing.

Because of Kennedy's campaign against the Mafia, Director Hoover was forced to sign on as well, signaling a change in the way crime business was done in America. In fact, the heat on organized crime became so intense that a number of bosses, including New Orleans thug Carlos Marcello, discussed assassinating President Kennedy in the hopes of getting rid of Bobby as AG. To this day, some believe that the Mafia had a hand in the murder of John Kennedy.

On the civil rights front, a great source of emotional information on the bloody and disgraceful resistance to African American rights can be found in the movie *Mississippi Burning*. If you have not seen that film, starring Gene Hackman, rent it right now.

As part of my historical source material collection, I own a letter written by Robert Kennedy to Louisiana Senator Allen Ellender, who was fighting hard to maintain the unfair racial status quo in the South. Ellender had challenged President Kennedy's order for the National Guard to restore order in Alabama after Governor George Wallace, a major Pinhead who repented before he died, refused a federal mandate to integrate the public schools in his state. On August 21, 1963, Attorney General Kennedy wrote this to Ellender:

> The cause for the call and use of the National Guard in Alabama was the obstruction of United States court orders for the entry of qualified students into the University of Alabama. On June 11, 1963, the President issued a proclamation commanding the governor of Alabama and all other persons engaged in the unlawful obstruction to cease and desist therefrom. When it appeared that the commands of that order had not been obeyed and the obstruction of justice was continuing, the President, on the same day, issued Executive Order 11111 authorizing and directing the secretary of defense to take all appropriate steps to remove obstructions of justice in the State of Alabama. . . .
>
> It is apparent that the Alabama National Guard was properly called into federal service. . . .

It should be noted here that President Eisenhower did not confront Alabama and some other states over their denial of rights to American citizens. But the Kennedy brothers did act decisively and succeeded in imposing justice where it had been denied for two centuries. Even though I generally respect Eisenhower, I simply can't understand his disdain for RFK, who did the right and courageous thing while Ike did not. Maybe that's it. Perhaps the old general knew he had failed blacks in the South and was galled that the young, arrogant Kennedys trumped him. That's pure speculation, but it's absolutely possible, is it not?

Office of the Attorney General
Washington, D. C.

OFFICE OF
RECEIVED
AUG 2 1 1963
ALLEN J. ELLENDER

Honorable Allen J. Ellender
United States Senate
Washington 25, D. C.

Dear Senator Ellender:

This is in response to your letter of July 22, 1963, enclosing a letter from Mr. Kenneth F. Bowen of LaFayette, Louisiana. Mr. Bowen inquired as to the legal authority under which the President acted recently to call the Alabama National Guard into federal service. In particular, he inquired why the call to federal service was not issued through the Governor of Alabama as provided in 10 U.S.C. § 3500. This was not done because the national guard units were called into federal service upon the basis of other statutory authority.

The cause for the call and use of the national guard in Alabama was the obstruction of United States court orders for the entry of qualified students into the University of Alabama. On June 11, 1963, the President issued a proclamation (No. 3542, 28 Fed. Reg. 5707) commanding the Governor of Alabama and all other persons engaged in the unlawful obstruction to cease and desist therefrom. When it appeared that the commands of that order had not been obeyed and the obstruction of justice was continuing, the President, on the same day, issued Executive Order 11111 (28 Fed. Reg. 5709) authorizing and directing the Secretary of Defense to take all appropriate steps to remove obstructions of justice in the State of Alabama. For this purpose he was authorized and directed inter alia, to call into the active military service of the United States, and use, any or all of the units of the Army National Guard or the Air National Guard of the State of Alabama. Both [...] executive order were issued un[...] the authority of sections 332, [...]

U.S. Code. Those provisions authorize the President, when faced with such unlawful obstructions against the authority of the United States as existed in Alabama, to "call into Federal service such of the militia of any State, and use such of the armed forces, as he considers necessary" (10 U.S.C. § 332) and to use "the militia or the armed forces, or both, or . . . other means" (10 U.S.C. § 333). The militia of the United States includes the national guard, meaning the Army National Guard and the Air National Guard of the several states. 10 U.S.C. § 311 and § 101 (9), (10), (12).

In furtherance of the President's order the Secretary of Defense immediately called into active military service all of the units and members of the Army National Guard and Air National Guard of the State of Alabama to serve in the active military service of the United States for an indefinite period and until relieved by appropriate orders. This call was transmitted by the Secretary of the Army, acting by direction of, and under delegation of authority from, the Secretary of Defense. Copies of the Department of the Army message (No. D.A. 340638, June 11, 1963) were furnished immediately to the Governor of Alabama and to the commanding officers of the Army National Guard and the Air National Guard of the State of Alabama.

It is apparent that the Alabama National Guard was properly called into federal service pursuant to 10 U.S.C. §§ 332-4, and in accordance with the procedure provided in those sections. Since the call to federal service did not invoke the authority of 10 U.S.C. § 3500, referred to by Mr. Bowen, the procedure prescribed by that section was not used.

I trust that the foregoing information will be of assistance to you.

Sincerely,

Attorney General

In this letter, RFK, a true champion of civil rights, defends the decision to send the National Guard to Alabama, where in one of the most historically Pinheaded moves ever, Governor George Wallace attempted to stop desegregation.

It is also interesting to note that the Kennedy brothers used the National Guard to protect American citizens from unfair behavior that harmed them. Do we not see a parallel to putting the Guard on the Southwestern border today? As mentioned earlier, I have been calling for that action during the past ten years because millions of Americans are being adversely affected by illegal alien chaos. So here's the question: Would Robert Kennedy have backed me on this? Impossible to call. Most committed liberals oppose taking strong action against illegal immigration. They see these poor immigrants as oppressed and in need of help, which indeed they are. But allowing federal immigration laws to be broken by millions of people is not a solution to anything and has caused considerable damage to America. Would RFK have seen that? I simply don't know.

Like his brother John, Robert Kennedy was a complicated man who did some bad things with his power as well. But the human condition dictates that we all do bad things on occasion. We all have balance sheets.

Robert Kennedy was a Patriot for understanding that evil, such as organized crime and institutional bigotry, cannot be allowed to stand unchallenged, especially in the noblest country in the world.

CÉSAR CHÁVEZ

Largely forgotten these days, Chávez was, in many ways, the Hispanic American equivalent to Dr. Martin Luther King Jr. In 1942 the high school dropout became a migrant worker and experienced the pain of brutal physical labor for incredibly low wages. Chávez then devoted his life to improving the lives of the mostly uneducated men and women working in the fields.

Using nonviolent methods, Chávez formed the United Farm Workers Union and as a result became a lightning rod of controversy. Accused by some of being a communist, the militant Chávez cultivated powerful people, including movie stars, and embarrassed many companies into upgrading benefits for migrant workers, at least somewhat.

Like Dr. King, César Chávez understood economic exploitation and was not an ardent capitalist. That alienated him from some Americans who might otherwise have admired his cause but felt his political leanings were too far Left. Be that as it may, the record shows that by sheer guts and determination, César Chávez helped millions of hard-working people improve their lives. For that alone, he was a Patriot.

JOHN EDWARDS

I know what you're thinking. Why bother? The guy defines the word Pinhead. His wife has cancer so he goes out and has an affair with a frenzied fan and winds up impregnating her. Then he lies about it on *Nightline*. Good grief. And this guy was a vice-presidential nominee? Paging John Kerry.

My primary beef with Edwards came before his cruel and outrageous personal conduct. As a candidate in the 2008 presidential primary sweepstakes, Edwards dishonestly used the plight of injured veterans in an effort to win votes.

You may remember that the former litigator ran around the country saying that there were hundreds of thousands of destitute vets living under bridges because they couldn't get jobs. Edwards wailed loudly about the apathy and injustice in America. How could we let this happen?

Well, we checked out the homeless "living under a bridge" claim and found it to be completely bogus. The Veterans Administration has enough beds to house almost every homeless vet in the United States. In fact, the VA will drive pretty much anywhere to pick up a vet who does not have shelter.

The truth is that a significant number of American veterans have substance abuse and mental health problems, just as a significant number of people in the general population do. These unfortunate citizens have a hard time functioning in a job situation and often wind up broke. Fox News military analyst Colonel David Hunt works with some of these vets in Boston, so I know the landscape. Edwards knew it, too. He just didn't care about the truth. He wanted to exploit the vets by demeaning the country, so he did. If you want to see the worst of America, catch up with John Edwards as he jogs back to his multimillion-dollar mansion in North Carolina. Don't even bother calling him a Pinhead. Don't talk to him at all. The man deserves total silence from his fellow citizens.

GEORGE SOROS

Here is another obvious Pinhead, but I just can't resist the opportunity to call attention to that fact once more.

Forbes magazine says the guy is worth $14 billion, and some estimate that he has spent $7 billion trying to impose his Far Left view on the world by funding despicable organizations like MoveOn.org. That was the outfit that accused General David Petraeus of betraying his country by successfully commanding the war in Iraq. The "General Betray Us" ad by MoveOn.org will live forever in infamy.

And so will George Soros. If you want the nuts and bolts on this guy, please read my book *Culture Warrior.* If you don't have the time, let me type up his résumé for you:

- is an atheist
- wants open borders for America
- wants to legalize narcotics
- convicted of felony insider trading by a French court
- through the Open Society Institute, which he founded,

gave $20,000 to defend attorney Lynne Stewart, who was
eventually convicted of assisting terrorists

- gamed U.S. election laws by donating close to $25 million
  to more than five hundred political organizations, all
  dedicated to humiliating President George W. Bush.

To be fair, Soros has given a good amount of money to help
people in need, but not nearly enough to buy his way out of Pinhead
status.

No, you're not seeing double. This
is one of my least favorite guys,
George Soros, in a shot that says to
me, "I'm twice the Pinhead most
people are!" What does it say to
you?

AS YOU MAY KNOW, I consider myself a warrior in the public arena.
But my position there does not even come close to the courage and
sacrifice of American military warriors. Let's take a look at some of
the famous and infamous Americans on the battlefield.

GENERAL GEORGE ARMSTRONG CUSTER

He was a crazy guy and most likely a Pinhead, but his loyal wife, Elizabeth, would have taken great issue with that. After Indians killed her husband, she traveled the country promoting his legacy and succeeded in making him a national hero whose name endures to this day.

After graduating dead last in his 1861 class at West Point, Custer demonstrated bravery as a cavalry officer in the Civil War and was promoted to brigadier general at age twenty-three. Catching the eye of General Grant, Custer participated in the last battle against General Lee as Confederate forces fled Richmond. The young Custer relished fighting, and that proved to be his undoing.

After the Civil War, Custer moved West and fought Indians, achieving some success in the campaign against the Cheyenne in 1868.

Eight years later, Custer was still at it, chasing the Sioux and Cheyenne into Montana. The rest, as they say, is history.

Ignoring orders to wait for reinforcements, Custer divided his men into three groups. His crew, numbering 266, attacked a sprawling Indian village inhabited by legendary warriors Sitting Bull and Crazy Horse. This did not turn out well. Thousands of Indians counterattacked, surrounding Custer and his troops in a field near the Little Big Horn River. The battle was brutal, with no survivors among Custer's troops. All the bodies were mutilated except for the general's, which the Indians left largely intact.

I have walked that battlefield and it is well worth doing. General Custer's arrogance killed him and his guys. The lesson for all of us is that if your head swells, somebody is sure to come along and knock it off. Custer felt he was invincible. Nobody is. He became a Pinhead and died from it.

GENERAL GEORGE PATTON

This man was truly a fascinating guy. Immortalized by actor George C. Scott in the movie *Patton*, the general was a lot like Custer but not quite so impetuous. He fought against Pancho Villa in Mexico, then alongside General John Pershing in World War I, where he was wounded twice and won a slew of medals. Patton continued his heroics in World War II, driving the Germans out of North Africa and Sicily. (He had a lot of help, of course.)

Then came General Patton's media moment. While visiting a hospital full of wounded GI's, he slapped one of them because he thought the man was malingering. The press went wild. It was a hundred times worse than the General Stanley McChrystal *Rolling Stone* incident. But unlike President Obama, who fired the unfortunate McChrystal, General Eisenhower did not sack Patton, who then went on to orchestrate great victories on French and German soil.

Was Patton a Pinhead for slapping the guy? Sure. No need to do that. If you think a soldier is faking an injury, investigate and, if he's guilty, cashier him. But a true leader should never show the lack of discipline that Patton demonstrated.

Unlike today, however, the press did not have enough power to get Patton fired, even though I believe many in the media wanted that to happen. Back in the 1940s, there was no television. The print press had some power and Patton did get hammered. But he survived and the United States was better for it.

So here's my question: Would President Obama have fired Patton? How about Presidents Bush-the-Younger or Bill Clinton? As we know, FDR deferred to Eisenhower, letting Ike keep his strongest field commander in place. I could be wrong, but I suspect that in today's America, Presidents Obama and Clinton would have sacked Patton. Bush is a wild card. He never cared much about what the press thought or even public opinion for that matter. So he might have kept Patton in place.

It is troubling that today, in a time of war, the media has so much power. A third-rate magazine like *Rolling Stone* should never have altered the course of the Afghan war, but it did. You may remember that many in the media called the firing of General McChrystal a "brilliant" move by the President. And with General David Petraeus now in charge in Afghanistan, that might turn out to be true. But the situation troubles me.

General Patton would have slapped silly the man who derailed McChrystal, writer Michael Hastings. Hastings is a Far Left zealot masquerading as a journalist. On my TV program, soldiers close to McChrystal said Hastings used "off-the-record" quotes to embarrass the general. Hastings denies that. I wasn't there, so I don't know. I *do* know, however, that Hastings is a rank Pinhead for being proud of destroying the general's career. Unfortunately, General McChrystal himself is a Pinhead for allowing a guy like that within a hundred yards of him. I mean, think about it. McChrystal served his country with courage and honor, yet a punk writer brings him down? Awful.

As for George Patton, he's obviously a Patriot. His skill and bravery helped defeat a tough enemy, the German army. That is a fact. And we should give Eisenhower credit for saving him.

AUDIE MURPHY

All Americans should know about this guy and, indeed, many do. His grave is the second most visited site at Arlington National Cemetery, only behind the eternal flame at John Kennedy's memorial shrine.

Born on a farm outside of Dallas, Texas, Murphy was drafted during World War II and assigned as a private to the Third Infantry Division. For three years, Murphy and the Third fought their way across Europe, experiencing some of the most hellacious combat ever known. Along the way, Murphy was wounded three times, killed approximately 240 enemy soldiers, and was decorated an astounding thirty-three times, including being awarded the Medal of Honor, our nation's highest award for bravery.

When the war ended, Murphy had been promoted to 2nd lieutenant and was a legend in America.

Here is a case where the press actually did its job. Audie Murphy's heroics were covered in detail, and his incredible courage was brought home in print for Americans to read and think about. It was a classic American story: a poor boy from Texas putting his life at risk countless times to defend his country from the vicious Third Reich. Does a news story get any better than that?

Well, no, not in this case. In fact, the story takes a turn for the worse. After the war, the legendary actor James Cagney invited Murphy to Hollywood. Because the ways of show business were alien to him, Murphy struggled to find his place in California. He became homeless, sometimes sleeping in a school gymnasium. In time, his fortunes changed, and Audie Murphy achieved movie stardom.

Murphy's 1949 rags-to-riches autobiography, *To Hell and Back,* became a bestseller and eventually was made into a movie starring the war hero himself. In a little-known fact, that film was the highest-grossing picture Universal released until *Jaws* came along in 1975. From there, Audie Murphy went on to make dozens of action movies, often portraying a cowboy, always playing the good guy.

Then life took another sad turn for Murphy. Suffering from post-traumatic stress disorder, he became addicted to sleeping pills. He kicked the habit by locking himself alone in a hotel room for a week. After that, he began publicizing the horrors that millions of combat veterans have experienced, bringing PTSD to the public's attention.

Audie Murphy was just an everyday guy. He had no advantages in life. He simply had courage. He exemplifies what Patriotism is all about. He put his life on the line for his country, then followed up by overcoming adversity and doing good things with his postwar life. Every school kid in America should know his story.

Lt. Audie L. Murphy of Farmersville, Texas, is pictured here receiving the Congressional Medal of Honor. He's a true Patriot who deserves as many badges for the things he accomplished *after* the war as for those he did during the war!

DAVY CROCKETT

Back in the 1950s, every kid learned the story of Davy Crockett, at least the Disney version of it. "Born on a mountaintop in Tennessee," the theme song began. And then actor Fess Parker, dressed entirely in buckskin, appeared on my small TV screen. To say I was mesmerized is a tremendous understatement. I was "all in" for Davy Crockett. I wore my coonskin cap all day. Only because my mother made me take it off to sleep did it ever leave my head (except for church). Thinking back, I believe that's why my hair is thinning today.

Walt Disney's Davy was a complete hero. He fought Indians, but only if they attacked him first. He killed bears, but only to get clothing (same thing with raccoons). He took on a variety of bad guys with help from his loyal sidekick, Georgy Russell (played by the Jeb Clampett guy, Buddy Ebsen). And, very sadly, Davy Crockett finally met his end, heroically defending the Alamo against the invading Mexican Army. All day long I sang, "Davy, Davy Crockett, king of the wild frontier."

But was he really the king of the wild frontier?

In 1814 the real-life Davy Crockett fought under Andrew Jackson at the battle of Horseshoe Bend, which pitted the U.S. military and its ally the Cherokee against the Creek tribe. The Creeks lost big-time.

However, sixteen years later, Jackson turned around and double-crossed the Cherokee people, forcing them to move off their land in the South and march west across the Mississippi. Crockett was a U.S. congressman at the time and voted against the Indian Removal Bill, a risky political move since anti-Indian sentiment was running high in America. Davy put his vote in no-spin terms:

> *Several of my colleagues told me that I was ruining myself. I told them I believed it was a wicked, unjust measure, and that I should go against it. Let the cost be to myself what it might . . . that I would sooner be honestly and politically damned, than hypocritically immortalized.*

Crockett's side lost in the House, and the terrible removal of the Cherokee commenced. But, obviously, he was a Patriot in his stand-up defense of the Indians.

As for the Alamo, it was a case of standing on principle again. Crockett and his 138 fellow defenders could have abandoned the San Antonio mission and lived to fight another day. They chose not to for a variety of reasons, with honor topping the list.

So while old Walt Disney went a bit overboard glamorizing Davy Crockett, he could have done worse. The man from Tennessee was a Patriot.

CHIEF JOSEPH

This is another warrior to whom time has not been kind. As the leader of the Nez Percé tribe in the Pacific Northwest, Joseph gave the U.S. Army all they could handle and did it with dignity. Unlike most other Indian leaders, he forbade his warriors to mutilate U.S. soldiers who were killed or captured in combat and strictly prohibited violence lodged against women and children.

In another of a long line of unfair impositions on the Indians, President Grant ordered the Nez Percé off their lands in 1877, directing the tribe to move to a government-controlled reservation in Idaho. Reluctantly, Chief Joseph commenced a fight.

Thus began a one-thousand-mile guerrilla war by the Nez Percé, who numbered just eight hundred. Soldiers sent to hunt the tribe down failed time after time. Finally, after three months of trying, U.S. forces trapped the Nez Percé in Montana near the Canadian border. Rather than see his people massacred, Joseph surrendered, saying, "From where the sun now stands, I will fight no more forever."

The chief lived for twenty more years watching his tribe slowly dissipate. That broke his heart. Joseph was a noble man and much more of a Patriot than many famous historical figures.

ANNIE OAKLEY

Somehow I've got to get a woman into the historical mix and Annie is my gal. How's this for a résumé: no education and no family life. In fact, she was institutionalized as a girl because her mother could not afford to raise her. When she finally got out of the brig, she became a child servant and was abused physically and mentally. It doesn't get much worse than that.

But wait a minute. Isn't a frothy musical play called *Annie Get Your Gun* based on Ms. Oakley's life? Yes, it is. But in reality, the play has little to do with the real Annie.

Born Phoebe Ann Mosey in Ohio on August 13, 1860, she stood just five feet tall, but could shoot a rifle better than almost anyone. Don't believe me? Annie could hit an airborne dime from ninety feet away. Try that sometime.

Even though her childhood was harsh, Ms. Oakley's spirit remained strong. For almost two decades she toured the country with Buffalo Bill (an uncouth wild man, by the way) and became one of the most famous women of her day. She was so beloved by her husband, Frank Butler, that after she died, he committed suicide by starving himself to death. Life was indeed tough back then.

For overcoming incredible obstacles and succeeding in a man's world, Annie Oakley was a Patriot.

BABE RUTH

Unquestionably the most famous baseball player of all time, Ruth might also have been the most talented man ever to play the game. Raised in a Catholic orphanage, Ruth demonstrated amazing natural athletic ability, and by his late teens he was pitching professionally, working his way to the Boston Red Sox. Then the Pinhead running the Red Sox sold him to the New York Yankees and there you go.

Ruth was so famous that during World War II, some Japanese troops in the Pacific yelled "to hell with Babe Ruth" as they charged into marine fire. Based on his lifestyle, hookers in all the American League cities might have yelled that as well because Ruth was a frequent customer. Problem is, he was married. Over the years his wife reportedly suffered greatly because of his indiscretions, which actually got him suspended from baseball for a time.

Despite his *Animal House* demeanor, Yankee Stadium in New York is still known as "the house that Ruth built," and there is no question that our national pastime came of age because the Babe hit so many dramatic home runs. But on balance, the guy was a cad whose unsavory activities were often covered up by corrupt sportswriters, some of whom actually accompanied him to the brothels. In my book, his talent doesn't mitigate his Pinhead status. When God blesses you with great talent, you owe Him something back.

NOW WE TURN to people who have made an impression during my lifetime. Most of these folks are icons and have become part of the American culture, for better or for worse. We begin with perhaps the most famous woman in the world, an incredible forty-eight years after her death.

MARILYN MONROE

Like Annie Oakley and Babe Ruth, Marilyn spent some time institutionalized as a child. Her mother, a single woman, had mental problems, and so little Norma Jeane Mortenson bounced from one foster home to another—twelve in all.

Undoubtedly, that affected Norma Jeane, who changed her name to Marilyn Monroe upon entering the shark-infested waters of Hollywood. For her entire adult life, Ms. Monroe led a turbulent existence, bouncing from one man to another before finally dying alone at age thirty-six from an overdose of pills.

Much has been written about Marilyn Monroe and her sensational private life. But that does not interest me much. If you have ever seen Marilyn in a movie, you know why so many people idolized her. Vulnerable yet beautiful, funny and charming, Ms. Monroe had charisma to burn. Perhaps never again will there be a movie star of this magnitude.

But, in the end, Marilyn squandered her talent and fame. Like Elvis Presley, perhaps the only star who has equaled Marilyn's screen presence, she simply could not handle the pressure of being someone adored by so many. On the set of her last released film, *The Misfits*, she was almost out of control from drugs and paranoia. Her costars, the veteran actors Clark Gable and Eli Wallach, felt helpless in trying to assist her. When I spoke with Mr. Wallach about the situation, he said it affected him deeply but by that point, she simply could not be reached.

So you might think that Marilyn Monroe deserves a Pinhead label for self-destructing. I'm not so sure. Like Babe Ruth, she brought joy to millions of folks who watched her movies. Unlike Ruth, she primarily hurt herself, not other people, at least as far as I can tell.

Therefore, for overcoming tremendous odds and achieving worldwide icon status, I am calling Marilyn Monroe a Patriot, with some reservations.

MADONNA

I don't know much about this one and care even less, but she did rise from working-class Detroit roots to worldwide icon status as well, so she's worth a few words.

Using sexual shock tactics combined with a few catchy tunes,

Madonna Louise Ciccone has become massively wealthy and hideously famous. That means that she has no life other than the one played out in front of the public. That is indeed hideous fame. Ask Elvis and Marilyn (if only we could).

But here's my measure on this. What exactly has Madonna done with all her money and notoriety? Yes, she has helped some charities (primarily in Africa), and once in a while she does a benefit for some kind of trendy cause, but not much else. Bono, for example, uses his money and clout to help people all over the world, as do many other celebrities. Not so much Madonna.

On a personal note, the faux English accent gets me. Here she is from the Motor City running around trying to sound like Princess Diana. She even moved to Great Britain for a while. What is that? So here's my talking points memo to Madonna:

America afforded you the opportunity to use your talent, and fate allowed you to rise from modest circumstances to wealth beyond comprehension. The United States gives opportunity to people like you and me to realize our dreams and potential. Nowhere on earth does the opportunity to pursue happiness exist on the level that America provides.

If you had been born in England, you would have been subjected to a class system that would have made your road much tougher. The Beatles proved it can be done, but by donning a phony British speech pattern and occasionally saying nasty things about your own country, you have become an embarrassment both to England and to the United States.

Also, you have achieved Pinhead status. And now you know why.

And that's the memo.

MEL GIBSON

What a shame. Here's a self-made guy who was once loved by millions all over the world for entertaining us with movies like *Braveheart* and *Lethal Weapon*. I met Gibson when he optioned my novel *Those Who Trespass* for a movie and enjoyed his company on a few occasions. He's basically a shy guy with an explosive amount of energy. Unharnessed, that energy has turned destructive.

Gibson's movie about the death of Jesus, *The Passion of the Christ*, made close to $1 billion worldwide but was vilified by many in the media. When I watched the film on the Fox movie lot in L.A. before it was released, I thought the violence was so explicit that it distracted from the overall story and told Gibson that. But I admired his take on good and evil and believe, to this day, that his faith in Jesus drove him to make this unforgettable film. I did not buy the accusations from some critics that the movie was intentionally anti-Semitic.

Then, in a drunk-driving incident, Gibson made some anti-Semitic remarks to a police officer. Not good.

Of course, the media flayed Gibson over that and, like his movie about Jesus, the intensive coverage was painful to watch. Whether it was overkill or not, I'll leave for you to decide, but please keep in mind the history of the Jewish people and how they have been brutalized. As with African Americans and Indians, Patriots should strive to understand that sensitivity is needed in certain situations involving groups of people who have been unfairly punished.

I lost contact with Mel Gibson after his bout with the legal system and was surprised to read that he broke up with his wife of twenty-nine years. Apparently, he then took up with some Russian woman and things got nasty with her. She secretly taped him saying more inappropriate things, including using the *n*-word to describe blacks.

There is no excusing any of this. Mel Gibson was admired by many but has squandered his talent and legacy in a series of Pinheaded moves. I have to tell you, though, it is painful to watch the public destruction of a human being. No one should be enjoying it.

JANIS JOPLIN AND JIM MORRISON

Now these were two screwed-up peas in a pod. Like Madonna, they both became famous in the music industry, rising to icon status in the 1960s.

Then they both used heroin to kill themselves.

The Port Arthur, Texas–born Joplin was buried at age twenty-seven after overdosing in Hollywood, a place that remains ground zero for self-destruction. Her best moments onstage came with her band Big Brother and the Holding Company, and Janis could definitely sing those blues. But it didn't really matter. Like so many other rock stars in the '60s, Janis embraced excess and degenerated into a complete mess. Was it her fault? Yeah, it was. Unlike Marilyn Monroe, she had a comfortable upbringing and could have led a rewarding life. But, no, she ingested massive amounts of chemicals until her body said "enough."

The same was true of Jim Morrison, the lead singer of The Doors. Blessed with great looks and one of the best rock voices of all time, Morrison never even paused at a rest stop on the highway of self-destruction. Like Joplin, he was found dead at age twenty-seven. He was lying in a bathtub in Paris, France. A postmortem cover-up took place, but authoritative sources say that heroin killed Morrison— no surprise because the guy took pretty much everything he could get his hands on. According to his bandmates, Morrison had even ingested drugs given to him by strangers without knowing what they were. No question, Morrison did not really care what happened to him. So he died.

I'm not sure which made a greater impact on our culture—this talented rock star's love of drugs or his love of music. As this museum exhibit suggests, he's still an influence on many today, for better or for worse.

The reason that I am including Janis Joplin and Jim Morrison in this book is that millions of young people all over the world idolized them and followed their lead into the world of drugs. I saw it up close and personal. Three of my boyhood friends died from drug addictions they acquired in the chaotic late 1960s. Rock stars in that era had a tremendous influence on the culture. I mean, few knew that Elvis Presley was a prescription drug junkie, but everybody knew that Joplin, Morrison, Jimi Hendrix, and legions of other rock performers were often stoned out of their minds. It was cool, far out. Like a band of demented pied pipers, these blanked-up rockers led many of their fans right into hell.

That's why they are Pinheads. And the same holds true for many stars in the music business today, especially rappers who peddle hate and debauchery. You guys are loathsome and destructive. And I'm calling you out!

ERROL FLYNN

Ever hear of this guy? He was a huge movie star in the 1940s who made the rock stars of the '60s look almost saintly.

Handsome and quick-witted on screen, he became world famous starring as Robin Hood and other action heroes. But behind the scenes this guy was completely out of control. In a huge national scandal, two teenaged girls accused him of statutory rape. The case actually went to trial and Flynn was acquitted. Based upon his subsequent activities, however, he was probably guilty. When he died from a heart attack at age fifty, he was having an affair with a fifteen-year-old girl. There's got to be a special place in hell for a guy like this.

Have you heard the phrase "in like Flynn"? That is Errol's legacy. Back then, the press would not expose guys like Flynn even though they knew he had a hard drug habit, a variety of venereal diseases, and was an all-around bad guy. Even my parents were fans. They had no idea what a disgraceful Pinhead the guy was. Now everybody knows.

LASSIE

I hated this show when I was a kid. I despised Timmy because the kid never did anything wrong, and I was in trouble all the time. I didn't care much about the dog, either, because my dog, Barney, had nothing in common with the heroic Lassie. If Barney saw you at the bottom of a well, you were toast unless you had a can of Alpo on you. Barney would walk away from anything that did not involve food. But if Lassie saw you down there in that well, the entire town would have mobilized within minutes.

True to the American spirit, Lassie could do anything! This beloved canine delivered ratings to CBS and quality entertainment to fans everywhere. Now with her own commemorative stamp, she's delivering the mail, too! Do you think I could get my own commemorative stamp someday?

In hindsight, I now realize that *Lassie*, the show starring the perfect collie who never pooped, served up valuable lessons for postwar America. Here on TV was an example of a loving family making a wholesome living on a farm someplace. They had a beautiful dog and harbored good feelings toward just about everybody. Can we send Eminem to Lassie's house?

There is something to be said for the TV programs of the 1950s and early '60s in which Ozzie and Harriet, David and Ricky, Dobie Gillis and Maynard, and the Cleaver family held court. Watching these programs as a kid made me feel good. Whatever was happening in my chaotic little world—and some of it was bad—those programs showed me that America was a nice, safe place where things always turned out well. Everybody loved everybody, and Lassie would never let you down.

And, so, the collie was a Patriot. Timmy, I'm not so sure about.

JACKIE ROBINSON, WILLIE MAYS, AND HANK AARON

Baseball saved me from the streets as a kid, and my favorite baseball player was number 24, Willie Mays, the centerfielder for the New York Giants.

But little did I know that Willie and other black players were going through hell on the diamond. When Jackie Robinson broke the color barrier with the Brooklyn Dodgers in 1947, he was subjected to hateful taunting every day he played. So were Willie Mays, Hank Aaron, and the other black players of the time. I love America, so when I think back on that kind of stuff, it makes me very sad.

To this day, I don't get it. Willie Mays was a genius on the field. He was excellent in every way. Why would anyone say anything mean to Willie? Or to Jackie? Or to Hank?

From my perch as a kid in the working-class suburb of Levittown, black people were just folks who lived a few miles away from me. My parents never said anything negative about them and supported my idolization of Willie Mays. In 1956 my father took me to the Polo Grounds and paid $3.50 apiece for two box seats so that we could be close to Willie when he slammed the ball out of the park. My dad even took home movies of him at the plate. I remember that like it was yesterday.

Willie Mays brought me more joy than even Davy Crockett. The guy motivated me to play ball all the time because I wanted to be like him. Because I was on the field all summer long as opposed to hanging around doing nothing, I avoided major trouble in a neighborhood full of it. So Willie Mays was more than just entertainment.

Baseball legend Hank Aaron (pictured here in the announcer's booth at the 2010 All-Star Game in Anaheim). This guy will always be an All-Star to me!

Just picture yourself trying to make a living in a high-pressure situation like that and having thousands of Pinheads cursing you just because of the color of your skin. Can you even process that? Every day that's what happened to black ballplayers in the land of the free and the home of the brave. But Willie Mays rarely complained. That, of course, annoyed the hell out of Jackie Robinson, who was much more assertive in dealing with the racism that came his way.

To me, Mays, Robinson, and Aaron were Patriots of the highest order. Because of their skill and willingness to suffer indignities, professional sports opened up to African Americans, who now dominate the playing fields and basketball courts of America. When a guy like LeBron James can become a page-one news story over his decision to play for the Miami Heat, it's clear how far we've come.

This subject is very personal with me. Sports saved me from going to some dark places. And Willie Mays was the centerpiece of that.

VIETNAM VETS

Finally in this chapter, I want to talk about Vietnam vets. Again, this is very personal to me. If you read my previous book, *A Bold Fresh Piece of Humanity,* you know that many guys in my neighborhood were drafted and assigned to fight in Vietnam. You also know that all of them came back to Levittown saying that the situation over there was chaotic and destructive. While some of my buddies worked it out, others did not. But all of those who saw combat in Vietnam have searing memories that will burden them forever.

Ray Cravens of Lebanon, Tennessee, wipes tears away as he and other Vietnam veterans are cheered during a ceremony welcoming them home in Fort Campbell, Kentucky, in August 2009. The ceremony was an official recognition of the sacrifice previous generations of soldiers, marines, sailors, and airmen made, many of whom received very little support following the war.

It's not like today when the United States has a professional, all-volunteer military. Back in the late 1960s, our country needed bodies to send to Southeast Asia because tens of thousands of bodies were coming back in bags. By all accounts, it was a brutal conflict that young men often entered into after just eight weeks of basic training. Eight weeks!

Fortunate guys like me could go to college and avoid the draft. But for those who did not pursue higher education, the draft board came knocking. After a national outcry that the poor were being discriminated against because of the college deferment deal, a lottery was instituted and random luck decided who was eligible to be drafted and who was not.

It is downright eerie how similar the current war in Afghanistan is to the Vietnam conflict. In both cases, we backed corrupt governments that do not and did not inspire confidence among the local population. In both cases, a brutal, totalitarian enemy that has time and terrain on its side faced our troops. The crucial difference is that America now has a motivated fighting force that is largely respected by the folks back home and even by the very liberal media. In Vietnam, that was certainly not the case.

As I mentioned earlier, Jane Fonda, a major Pinhead player, epitomizes what went on back then. A very pretty young actress, Fonda was strident and stupid in her support of the Viet Cong and North Vietnamese. She even traveled to Hanoi, allowing herself to be used by the oppressive and brutal Ho Chi Minh regime. You may remember pictures of Jane sitting atop a North Vietnamese anti-aircraft gun while, just a few miles away, captured American servicemen like John McCain were being tortured in small cells. Fonda wasn't the only shameful celebrity who committed treason or crossed a fine line. Actor Donald Sutherland and a variety of rock idiots did so as well. But no one disgraced her country more than Jane Fonda.

The politics of the war are well known to anyone who cares. The conflict destroyed the presidency of Lyndon Johnson and the lives of millions of human beings, including hundreds of thousands of Americans either killed or injured in the theater of war. The U.S. military was never defeated on the battlefield, but our national will flagged, and understandably so. Some wars are simply not worth the blood and treasure. Vietnam was one of them. Iraq was another.

Whenever I meet a Vietnam vet, I thank them for their patriotism. Overwhelmingly, these brave men and women served their country in a time of crisis and served well. My cousin, Dickie Melton, was as brave a man as ever walked point in a dark jungle. He lived to tell about it, but it took a tremendous toll on him. When I asked Dick if he regretted going to Vietnam, he didn't pause. "Because of me there are some names not on that wall [the Vietnam Memorial in Washington honoring the dead]," he said. "So it was worth it."

Dickie Melton exemplifies the sacrifice that all Vietnam vets made. I previously said that all American schoolchildren should know about Audie Murphy's heroism. Well, they should also know about the ordeal of the Vietnam veteran. We need to honor these guys and gals and, perhaps, even apologize to them. They were Patriots while many of us were unappreciative or even downright nasty about their service to our country. That historical wrong needs to be righted. While Jane Fonda made millions after her disgraceful conduct, most Vietnam vets returned home to make modest livings and are reminders that life, indeed, is not fair.

The Vietnam vet is a true American icon. I'm glad that I could spotlight that in these pages.

★

CHAPTER 10

The Last Word

This is the end, my only friend, the end.

—*The Doors*

SO I'VE DECIDED TO END this book with a look back at my big inter-view with then-Senator Barack Obama during the 2008 presidential campaign. I think the conversation is interesting because, by exam-ining the Q and A, we can see what he said during the campaign, and then compare his words with what he's actually done as President. After key passages of the interview, you'll see that I've provided some analysis in the gray-shaded boxes. Should be fun.

The backstory of this interview, which took place in York, Penn-sylvania, on September 4, 2008, is fascinating. As you may remem-ber, candidate Obama had promised to come on the *Factor* after I cornered him in New Hampshire in January 2008.

The confrontation itself received national attention because I shoved one of Obama's advance men. Although the action made me look like a fool to some, I had to get physical because the guy was blocking my cameraman from shooting Senator Obama as he worked the rope line after a speech. With my microphone on, I asked the guy, who happened to be six-eight, to stop "blocking the shot." When he did not, I physically removed him from camera range. For my detractors, that just reinforced my image as a thuggish lout. For my supporters, it was another sign that no one will inhibit the *Factor* from covering events. No one.

After the shove, the Secret Service, clearly not wanting any part of the situation, let me approach then-Senator Obama, and with the camera rolling, I asked him when he was coming on the *Factor*. He said it would be after the primaries. And he kept his word.

But the Obama campaign was smart about the timing. Because they knew the *Factor* was in Minnesota, covering the Republican Convention, and that millions of Americans would be watching that coverage, they waited until the convention was actually under way before calling us about the interview. They told us we had just hours to get from St. Paul, where John McCain and Sarah Palin were holding court, to central Pennsylvania. The Obama guys knew that an interview on the *Factor* would garner major attention—and it did.

Not surprisingly, some GOP viewers criticized me for interrupting their party's coverage and going to York, Pennsylvania. But for us, that was the bigger news story. Besides, my Fox News colleagues had the convention well covered.

The Obama campaign gave us thirty minutes with the senator, and I think we used the time wisely. See if you agree.

Then-Senator Barack Obama with me on the *Factor*. I don't think we had gotten to the part where I was giving him jazz about basketball yet.

SENATOR OBAMA'S SEPTEMBER 2008 INTERVIEW ON *THE O'REILLY FACTOR*

Complete, Unabridged, and Annotated Transcript

Bill O'Reilly: Well, first of all, thanks for being a man of your word—

Sen. Barack Obama: You bet.

O'Reilly: —but I was worried there for a while. . . .

Obama: [*Laughs.*]

O'Reilly: It's been nine months since we, uh, last met—

Obama: Yes.

O'Reilly: —in, uh, New Hampshire. . . .

Obama: It took a little while. I had, I have had a few things to do—

O'Reilly: Well, I understand, yeah.

Obama: But I, but I. . . . And I appreciate your having me on the show.

O'Reilly: Okay. Let's start with national security. Do you believe we are in the middle of a war on terror?

Obama: Absolutely.

O'Reilly: Who is the enemy?

Obama: Al-Qaeda, the Taliban, a whole host of networks that are bent on, uh, attacking America; who have a distorted ideology; who have perverted the faith of Islam. And so we have to go after them.

O'Reilly: Is Iran part of that component?

Obama: Iran is a major threat. Now I don't think that there is a—that they are not part of the same network; yeah, you have got Shia and you have got Sunni. And so, Iran. . . . The threat we have is with Hezbollah, Hamas—

O'Reilly: But they are behind—they are, they are fueling the—

Obama: They, they—they have fueled a whole host of terrorist organizations—

O'Reilly: Mm-hmm.

Obama: My only point is that, we have got to be absolutely clear that Shia terrorists may not be the same—

O'Reilly: But they are the same war on terror, right?

Obama: —of what we have to battle, which is—those who are trying to do us harm. My only point is that we have got to have, uh, the ability to distinguish between these groups. Because, for example, the war, uh . . . the war in Iraq is a good example—where I believe the administration lumped together Saddam Hussein—a terrible guy—with al-Qaeda, which had nothing to do with Saddam Hussein—

O'Reilly: All right. So we'll get to that in a minute—

Obama: And as a consequence, we ended up, uh—I think—misdirecting our resources. So they are all part of various terrorist networks that we have to shut down and we have to destroy, but they may not all be part and parcel of the same ideology.

O'Reilly: But I still don't understand—and I am asking this as an American, as well as a journalist—well, how threatening do you feel Iran is?

Obama: See, look, I think. . . . And I think—

O'Reilly: If Iran gets a nuclear weapon, okay?

Obama: Mm-hmm.

O'Reilly: To me, they are gonna give it to Hezbollah, if they can develop the technology. Well, why not? And, and then so we don't have anything to do with it.

Obama: Yeah.

O'Reilly: So therefore, the next President of the United States is going to have to make a decision—

Obama: Right.

O'Reilly: About Iran, whether to stop them militarily. Because I don't believe. . . . If diplomacy works, fine; but you have got to have a plan B. And, and a lot of people are saying, "Look, Barack Obama is not going to attack Iran."

Obama: Well, here, here, here—here is where you and I agree. It is unacceptable for Iran to possess a nuclear weapon. It's a game changer—and I have said that repeatedly. I have also said I would never take a military option off the table.

O'Reilly: But would you prepare for one?

Obama: Well. . . . Listen—

O'Reilly: Answer the question, Senator.

Obama: No. No, that—

O'Reilly: Anybody can "option." But would you prepare for it?

Obama: Look, it is not appropriate for somebody—who is one of two people who could be the President of the United States—to start tipping their hand in terms of what their plans might be with respect to Iran. It's sufficient to say I would not take the military option off the table, and that I will never hesitate to use our military force in order to protect the homeland and the United States' interests. But—where I disagree with you, is the notion that we have exhausted every other resource. Because the fact of the matter is, is that for six, seven years during this administration, we weren't working close—as closely as we needed to with the Europeans to, to—

O'Reilly: All right.

Obama: —to create—

O'Reilly: Diplomacy might work—

Obama: —to, to—

O'Reilly: You might be able to sanction economically. . . .

Obama: Sanctions—sanctions. . . .

O'Reilly: Maybe.

Obama: Maybe.

O'Reilly: But that's, that's all hypothetical.

Obama: But, but what? Everything is hypothetical. But the question is—are we trying to do what we need to do to ratchet up the pressure on them to change their—

O'Reilly: Okay. We'll assume that you are gonna ratchet everything you could ratchet up. But I am going to assume that Iran is gonna say, "Blank you, we are gonna do what we want."

Obama: Yeah. [*Laughs.*]

O'Reilly: And I want a President—whether it's you or McCain—who says—

Obama: Right.

O'Reilly: "You ain't doing that."

Obama: Okay.

> So what's happened since this interview? Iran has continued to develop its nuclear weapons program despite threats and overall angst by many people who understand the dangers of having killers with no conscience possessing nukes. After a year and a half in office, President Obama was finally able to get some sanctions placed on that country, primarily freezing Iranian assets abroad, limiting

oil sales, and preventing Iranian banks from doing business internationally.

But is there anyone on earth who really thinks that these sanctions are going to stop the nutty mullahs from making a nuclear weapon? Anyone? Al Franken?

No, Iran will suffer some financial inconvenience but still produce those nukes so that they can threaten other countries with them—and perhaps also develop a nasty "dirty bomb" to be handed over to a terrorist kill team.

In other words, we are in exactly the same place with Iran that we were two years ago when I spoke with the President. If Barack Obama has a "plan B," it is being kept well under wraps. As you just read, he did not want to tip his hand back then, nor is he tipping it now. The result: Iran will get a nuclear weapon soon. The only thing that could prevent that from happening is an Israeli military strike to destroy the Iranian nuclear facilities. But the consequences of an attack on Iran would be bloody and severe, perhaps even leading to a world war. That's what is keeping Obama from setting up any strong backup plans like a naval blockade. The nasty mullahs well understand that America and most other nations do not want the world economy devastated by violence. So they confidently continue enriching uranium, daring the world to stop them.

O'Reilly: All right, let's go to Iraq. I think history will show it's the wrong battlefield, okay? And I think that you were perspicacious in your original assessment of the battlefield.

Obama: And I appreciate that.

O'Reilly: But I think you were desperately wrong on the surge. And I think you should admit it to the nation, that now we have defeated the terrorists—in Iraq—and they—that al-Qaeda came there, after we invaded—as you know, okay?

Obama: Right. Absolutely right.

O'Reilly: And we defeated them.

Obama: Right.

O'Reilly: If we didn't, they would have used it as a staging ground.

Obama: Yes.

O'Reilly: We have also inhibited Iran from controlling the southern part of Iraq—by the surge—which you did not support. So why won't you say, "I was right in the beginning, and I was wrong about that"?

Obama: You know, if, if you have, if you have listened to what I have said—and I'll, and I'll repeat it right here on this show—I think that there is no doubt that the violence is down. I believe that that is a testimony to the troops that were sent and General Petraeus and Ambassador Crocker. I think that the surge has succeeded . . . in ways that nobody anticipated—by the way, including President Bush and the other supporters. Now, it has gone very well, partly because of the Anbar situation—

O'Reilly: The awakening, right.

Obama: —and the, the Sunni awakening—partly because the, the Shia—

O'Reilly: Well, if it were up to you, there wouldn't have been a surge—

Obama: Well, look—

O'Reilly: No, no, no, no.

Obama: No, no, no, no. No, no, no, no.

O'Reilly: Look, if it were up to you, there wouldn't have been a surge.

Obama: No, no, no, no.

O'Reilly: You and Joe Biden—

Obama: No.

O'Reilly: —no surge.

Obama: Hold on a second, Bill. If you look at the debate that was taking place, we had gone through five years of mismanagement of this war that I thought was disastrous. And the President wanted to double down and continue on an open-ended policy that did not create the kinds of pressure on the Iraqis to take responsibility and reconcile—

O'Reilly: Well—

Obama: Well, look, that—

O'Reilly: Come on—

Obama: Well, what I have said is—I have already said, it's succeeded beyond our wildest dreams.

O'Reilly: Right. So why can't you just say, "I was right in the beginning, and I was wrong about the surge"?

Obama: Because there is an underlying problem with what we have done. We have reduced the violence—

O'Reilly: Yeah?

Obama: But the Iraqis still haven't taken responsibility. And we still don't have the kind of political reconciliation. That we are still spending, Bill, $10 to $12 billion a month—

O'Reilly: And I hope that, if you are President, you can get them to kick in and pay us back. And I'll—and I'll go with you.

Obama: Let's go.

O'Reilly: We'll get some of that money back.

Obama: Yeah. [*Laughs.*]

O'Reilly: All right, let's go to Afghanistan.

Obama: All right.

O'Reilly: Look, there is no winning the Taliban war—

Obama: Yes?

O'Reilly: —unless Pakistan cracks down on the guys that are in—Pakistan, okay?

Obama: And you and I agree completely.

O'Reilly: Okay, yeah? And we all know that.

Obama: Right.

O'Reilly: You gave a speech in Denver—a good speech, by the way.

Obama: Thank you.

O'Reilly: But you bloviated about McCain not following them into the cave. You are not going to invade Pakistan, Senator, if you are President. You are not gonna send ground troops in there, and you know it.

Obama: Here, here, here is, here is the problem. John McCain loves to say, "I will follow 'em to the gates—to the gates of hell."

O'Reilly: But he is not going to invade either.

Obama: Well, that—and, and the point is, what he—what we could have done is—

O'Reilly: No, no, not "could." Let's—what do we do now?

Obama: What, what we can do—

O'Reilly: Yeah?

Obama: —is stay focused on Afghanistan—

O'Reilly: Yeah?

Obama: —and put more pressure on the Pakistanis.

O'Reilly: Like what?

Obama: Well, for example, we are providing them military aid, without having enough strings attached. So they are using the military that we use—

O'Reilly: For nothing.

Obama: —for—to Pakistan. They are—they are preparing for a war against India.

O'Reilly: So you are gonna pull them out, and let the Islamic fundamentals take 'em over?

Obama: No, no, no, no. What we say is, "Look, we are gonna provide them with additional, uh, military support—targeted at terrorists. And we are gonna help build their democracy and provide—"

O'Reilly: That's exactly what we are doing now—

Obama: —the kind of funding—

O'Reilly: Right.

Obama: But, but we are not—

O'Reilly: —and he is doing that now.

Obama: We, we haven't—that's not what we have been doing, Bill. We have wasted $10 billion with Musharraf without holding him accountable for knocking out those people.

O'Reilly: All right. So you are gonna—again—more diplomacy—and we need it, absolutely. Try to convince the Pakistani government to take a more aggressive approach—

Obama: And what I would, and what I would—

O'Reilly: —and, and to say, "If you don't, we will pull the plug."

Obama: And, and what I will do is—well, if we have bin Laden in our sights—

O'Reilly: Yeah?

Obama: —we target him, and we knock him out.

O'Reilly: But everybody would do that.

Obama: Well, I mean—

O'Reilly: I mean, that would be the biggest win Bush could have—

Obama: Of course.

O'Reilly: —is if we could do that.

Obama: And that is—

O'Reilly: But you can't send these ground troops in, because then all hell breaks loose—

Obama: We can't—we, we—we can't have, uh, uh. . . . That nobody talked about some full-blown invasion of Afghanistan. But the simple point that I made was, we have got to put more pressure on Pakistan—to do what they need to do.

O'Reilly: I mean, well, I gotta tell you. I don't—I don't think the administration—

Obama: I don't think, I don't think you and I disagree on this.

O'Reilly: No, but they have put an enormous amount of pressure. And NATO doesn't fight in, uh, in Afghanistan—I don't know whether you know that or not.

Obama: Well, first—

O'Reilly: The Germans won't fight.

Obama: Well—

O'Reilly: The French will, because of Sarkozy.

Obama: They will. They—

O'Reilly: But the Germans wouldn't allow it, and the others won't.

Obama: Right.

O'Reilly: So it's all on us, again. Why? Well, why won't the Germans fight against the Taliban?

Obama: Well, you know part of the reason?

O'Reilly: What?

Obama: Part of the reason is, is that we have soured our relationship—with the Europeans—after Iraq. And you know, when I went over to Europe . . . and if you listen to that speech in Berlin—which you know, a lot of your buddies had a good time making fun of—

O'Reilly: I don't have any buddies, but— [*Laughs.*]

Obama: [*Laughs.*] But if, if you listen to what I said, one of the things I said in that speech is, "You cannot think that the Americans are gonna just carry all the weight on this thing. You guys have to step up to the plate."

O'Reilly: So when you are President—?

Obama: But, but Bob Gates, the secretary of defense—who, by the way, I think is a, is a serious guy in this administration and has, and has helped—

O'Reilly: A good guy.

Obama: —helped, helped straighten out some of the foreign policy problems—he himself has acknowledged that part of the problem is, politically, there is, uh—there is enough anti-Iraq sentiment in there—in, in Europe—

O'Reilly: —to poison the well for Afghanistan.

Obama: —to poison the well for Afghanistan.

O'Reilly: So you are gonna change all that with a magic wand? Come on.

Obama: I am not gonna—no, I am not gonna—no, I am not gonna change all that with a magic wand. That, that—I am not gonna change anything with a magic wand. What I am gonna

do is I am gonna, uh, engage in the kind of liberal diplomacy—
and change our policy in Iraq to send a signal to the world, the
central front on terror right now is in Afghanistan, and the
hills between Pakistan and Afghanistan.

O'Reilly: Yeah, but you can't, you can't change a thing in Iraq,
uh, uh, if it's gonna benefit Iran. And, and that's—

Obama: Yeah, that I agree with you.

O'Reilly: That's gonna be your minefield as you go on—

Obama: But, but Bill, uh, you and I probably agree on the fact
that Iran is one of the biggest beneficiaries of us going into the
Iraq in the first place—

O'Reilly: It has been, but not now. Now, now they are paying a
big price for miscalculating—

Obama: Well—

O'Reilly: —the resolve of our country.

Obama: I, I will say that the, that the fact that the Shia militias
have folded up—right now—is a good thing.

> Where do I start with this? First of all, that was the only
> time so far that I have heard President Obama admit he had
> made a mistake. As you see, he said the surge worked, but he,
> of course, had forcefully opposed it. Two years ago, that was
> the big headline that came out of this interview.
>   Because Iraq remains an unstable situation, the
> President has been patient in withdrawing U.S. troops from
> this troubled country. That measured policy has angered the
> Far Left. I think we should give Mr. Obama credit for not
> caving into that constituency, which is misguided on Iraq. In
> light of all the blood and treasure the United States has spent

there, we simply cannot let Iraq go down the drain. But we should never again get involved in this kind of morass.

As for Afghanistan, it's obviously a colossal mess. But, do you know what? That's nobody's fault. The place is just impossible. About ten years ago, American Special Forces and some Afghan allies defeated the thuggish Taliban in about ten minutes. Since then, the situation has deteriorated into an absolute debacle.

After a decade of our involvement, most Afghan police are arrogantly corrupt, the army rarely fights, and the President of Afghanistan, Hamid Karzai, is an incompetent weakling who is probably a criminal. Certainly, his brother, who runs the province of Kandahar, is a thief and a drug lord. Just as President Bush was before him, President Obama is stymied. The Taliban, hiding in plain sight by dressing in civilian clothing, are able to kill at will, terrorizing the population at night. NATO forces, no matter how brave and skilled, can't protect the Afghan people because there are not enough NATO forces. That means that the poor Afghani folks are afraid to support the Americans and NATO, which could mean death even though the allies are sincerely trying to help them and deny the terrorists an important sanctuary.

The Taliban can also hide out in Pakistan, and NATO forces can't cross the border to kill them. In addition, some Pakistani intelligence big shots are actually supplying the Taliban with arms and logistics. Can you say *chaos?*

In a controversial move, President Obama took months to announce his decision to send more troops to Afghanistan but simultaneously undermined this move by promising to begin pulling U.S. forces out of there in July 2011. On hearing that, the Taliban broke out some humus and pita bread, or whatever it is they eat, and celebrated.

Then the Afghan commander, General McChrystal, got sandbagged by the dopes at *Rolling Stone,* and the world finally focused on what is an awful situation.

We should all be praying that General David Petraeus can pull off another miracle in Afghanistan and stabilize the country. If he does not do that, the Taliban will continue to brutalize millions of innocent people (especially women), and al-Qaeda terrorists will once again have room to roam. Remember, the reason NATO is in Afghanistan at all is because the Taliban partnered up with al-Qaeda before the attacks on 9/11. Nothing much has changed in that relationship.

If NATO fails in Afghanistan, the defeat will be on President Obama. It is his war now, just as Vietnam became LBJ's war, even though that war began under President Kennedy. I believe President Obama realizes the danger to him here. That means General Petraeus will get what he needs to do what he does. But this thing is hanging by a thread; absolutely anything could happen. In fact, Michael Scheuer, a former CIA agent who headed the bin Laden unit, writes that the Afghan war is already lost:

"Afghans hate and will not tolerate their country being occupied by foreigner infidel." This [historic quote] is verifiable over almost 24 centuries of history by referring to the Afghan experiences of Alexander the Great, the British Empire, and the Soviet Union. It took varying periods for the Afghans to get rid of each occupier—the Greeks were particularly tough to root out as Alexander created Greek colonies in the country— but in time each was defeated and left with its tail between its legs. And so will we.

Mr. Scheuer is a noninterventionist and skews his commentary that way, but there is no question that President Obama's strategy of limited engagement while winning Afghan hearts and minds may not work. Scheuer is blunt on the point:

War means fighting, and fighting means killing, and any other approach to war means wasted resources and lives, and will yield nothing but defeat and the need to fight the same war over again. This is why Obama should have sent a marine [commander] to replace [General] McChrystal. This is also why he did not.

Finally, I get a ton of mail basically agreeing with Michael Scheuer and also arguing that the President is soft on terrorism in general. Some of the correspondents point to the fact that the President will not even use the words "war on terror." True, but another fact defines Mr. Obama as the "drone king." In his pursuit of terrorists, he has ordered scores of missile attacks launched from Predator drones. They have been devastatingly effective, killing hundreds of al-Qaeda and Taliban leaders along with some civilians. Obama has used this space-age weapon far more than President Bush did. So how do we explain that? If he's soft on terrorism, why is he conducting a very aggressive missile campaign, which by the way the ACLU and other Far Left kooks hate? That's an interesting question, is it not? Remember, President Obama is a complicated guy. One of the major themes of this book is that things are not always what they seem. I give a lot of credit to CIA Chief Leon Panetta, a true Patriot, for wising up Mr. Obama about the threat these terrorist killers pose to Americans. So the next

time you hear that Mr. Obama is a Pinhead for not taking
the war on terror seriously enough, remember that he is
definitely the "drone king."

O'Reilly: Okay. Uh, United States and Poland, putting the
missile shield in Poland.

Obama: Mm-hmm.

O'Reilly: All right? Putin doesn't like it.

Obama: Right.

O'Reilly: Are you gonna keep that missile shield in there?

Obama: I think that we have to make sure that, uh, uh—and
I have said this before. The Russians are playing a game, and
they pretend that this missile shield is directed against all their
interests.

O'Reilly: Yeah, it's ridiculous. It's a defensive thing.

Obama: It's, it's a defensive thing. And we—

O'Reilly: So you are gonna keep it there then?

Obama: And, and given, given what has happened in Georgia,
I think that we have to send a clear signal that Poland and
other countries in that region are, are not gonna be subject to
intimidation and aggression—

O'Reilly: Okay, so I just want to get this on record. If you are
elected President, you are keeping the missile shield in Poland?

Obama: I believe that the missile shield is appropriate. I want to
make sure it works, though. I want to make sure it works.

O'Reilly: Well, we are testing—

Obama: And that's one of the problems that we have got.

O'Reilly: So Putin, uh, comes out last week and he says, "Hey look, uh, we are gonna reimpose our dominance on all of the countries that surround us. And we don't care whether you like it or not, because you are tied down in Afghanistan—Iraq and Afghanistan—and we are gonna do what we want to do."

Obama: Sure.

O'Reilly: Such a nasty little guy, number one.

Obama: [*Laughs.*]

O'Reilly: And would you agree with that assessment?

Obama: [*Laughs.*] Well, that—I'll agree with the assessment that, uh—I wouldn't look into his soul and, uh—

O'Reilly: Yeah.

Obama: —and think I know him.

O'Reilly: And I'll put a cowboy hat on the guy.

Obama: Yes.

O'Reilly: This is gonna be a problem, all right?

Obama: Oh, this is a huge problem.

O'Reilly: Okay. And, and you are gonna have to confront Putin—

Obama: And we are going to—and that's exactly right.

O'Reilly: Maybe not militarily, and maybe you can do it other ways. But Europe is weak and Europe is cowardly—

Obama: Right.

O'Reilly: You know, what are they gonna have? Another meeting? Yeah, Putin is quaking, aren't they? Isn't Putin quaking about that? They are gonna have another meeting—

Obama: Well, you know what? And here, here, here is the one thing I would say. . . . There are, there are two things where we can have some leverage over Russia. Number one is that, commercially, they are tied up with Europe, and they are increasingly integrating. Their stock market has taken a beating since they went into Georgia.

O'Reilly: Yes.

Obama: But that—

O'Reilly: Like they care.

Obama: Well, Putin may not care, but there are a whole bunch of folks that are—

O'Reilly: They do. Right.

Obama: There are a whole bunch of millionaires in Moscow who do care, all right? So that's a leverage point. And the Europeans can be helpful in applying that leverage point, and that's point number one. The second thing that we have to do is actually defensive: We have got to get our energy policy straight. As long as they are getting over $100 a barrel for oil, then they are gonna be able to act—and that's the biggest problem we have.

On September 17, 2009, President Obama announced that the United States would scrap the planned missile defense shield for Poland and the Czech Republic. Notice in the interview that Mr. Obama said the missile shield was "appropriate," but that it has to "work." He did not swear he would keep it. He danced.

President Barack Obama, Russian President Dmitry Medvedev (*left*), and Czech Republic President Václav Klaus (*center right*) share a toast at a luncheon before signing the New Start START Treaty on April 8, 2010. So what exactly are we celebrating?

The President gave into Vladimir Putin's paranoia about the shield because he wanted the wily Russian leader to lay off Georgia and Ukraine. This was one of those Chicago backroom deals. Putin got the shield shelved; Obama got less aggressive Russian military expansion. Poland and the Czechs got hosed.

Welcome to the real world.

Republicans, of course, screamed about the President's "sell-out" to Putin, but since the situation is below the radar (sorry), most Americans couldn't care less about it.

For the record, the Obama administration says it isn't giving in to Russian demands; it is just shifting the missile

strategy around. According to Secretary of Defense Robert
Gates, a Patriot, the United States will now deploy Navy
Aegis ships equipped with SM-3 interceptor missiles in the
eastern Mediterranean Sea in order to block any aggressive
action by Iran. Down the road, Gates says, the United States
might install the interceptors in Poland and the Czech
Republic as well.

Again, few of your fellow citizens care about this. If you
do, you can make the call as to whether or not it's a Pinhead
move.

O'Reilly: Yeah, let's get to the economy. I want you to react to a
couple of steps that I, that I pulled outta here. You are a big "tax
the rich" guy.

Obama: [*Laughs.*] Yeah.

O'Reilly: Aren't you?

Obama: Just you, Bill.

O'Reilly: I know.

Obama: I think you are making too much money.

O'Reilly: You and Hillary both, you just want to take my
money.

Obama: [*Laughs.*]

O'Reilly: And you can have it; I mean, I don't care if I live in a
hut.

Obama: [*Laughs.*]

O'Reilly: All right. And you want to "tax the rich." Under
President Bush—

Obama: Yes.

O'Reilly: —the government—the federal government derived 20 percent more revenue than under President Clinton. Did you know that?

Obama: Well, the, uh—

O'Reilly: Did you know that?

Obama: The, the economy grew, Bill.

O'Reilly: It grew. That's right.

Obama: The economy grew, so—

O'Reilly: Under President Bush—

Obama: —so, so of course, uh, the, uh, the—

O'Reilly: —the, the economy grew 19 percent more than Clinton.

Obama: Right.

O'Reilly: See, this is what I am not getting about you Democrats—

Obama: No. No, no, no, no. Hold on, Bill.

O'Reilly: Nineteen percent—

Obama: Wait, wait, wait, wait. Don't, don't—hold on a second now. I mean, because you know, you, you, you—you know the famous saying about "There are—there are lies, damn lies, and statistics"?

O'Reilly: Yeah.

Obama: I mean, well, you and I can—we can play a statistics game—

O'Reilly: I know, I know it's bull—I know it is—

Obama: So, so, so what. . . . Well, let's, let's, let's be clear on the record, all right?

O'Reilly: All right.

Obama: The, uh. . . . During the Bush administration—

O'Reilly: Yeah?

Obama: —there was economic growth. Not as fast as during the 1990s, okay, but there was growth during the Bush administration. But what happened was, that wages and incomes—for ordinary Americans—the guys who watch your show—

O'Reilly: Yeah.

Obama: —the guys who you advocate for and you speak for on this show—

O'Reilly: Right.

Obama: —their wages and incomes did not go up.

O'Reilly: Why?

Obama: They went, they went down.

O'Reilly: Do you know why?

Obama: And the reason they went down—

O'Reilly: Yeah?

Obama: —is because most of the corporate profits and increased productivity went to the top—not just 1 percent—but the top one-tenth of 1 percent.

O'Reilly: All right. Let me submit to you that you are wrong—

Obama: And as part of, as part of—

O'Reilly: Let me submit to you that you are wrong, okay?

Obama: Right, okay, make your argument.

O'Reilly: We have been studying this issue—because we want to be fair and balanced and give all sides.

Obama: Right.

O'Reilly: The reason the wages have been depressed—and they are not that much: it's about four or five hundred dollars, uh, for the Bush administration, real wages up; and about two thousand under the Clinton administration—is because there are 10 million immigrants—new immigrants—in the workforce—most of whom are illegal aliens.

Obama: Bill—

O'Reilly: Those 10 million—

Obama: —I totally disagree with you—

O'Reilly: —with their, with their salaries—

Obama: Yeah?

O'Reilly: —have brought it down. But again, that's statistics, yes.

Obama: But, but, but, but—

O'Reilly: But let's get back to "tax the rich."

Obama: All right, but, but what—so let me just finish making my point.

O'Reilly: All right.

Obama: The fact is, for people in your income bracket—and mine—

O'Reilly: Right.

Obama: Now, we, we, we both come from humble beginnings and we worked our—and we were talking before the show. And the fact that, only in America, could we have this success.

O'Reilly: Absolutely.

Obama: And, and I—and I am not somebody who begrudges that success. I want people to—

O'Reilly: But you want 50 percent of my success—

Obama: No, I don't want it—

O'Reilly: Yeah, you do.

Obama: No, I don't—

O'Reilly: That's your tax rate.

Obama: That is not true—

O'Reilly: Fifty.

Obama: What I am—

O'Reilly: Fifty.

Obama: What, what I have said is, is that, uh, uh. . . . Now let's be clear about this—

O'Reilly: Payroll tax and, and income tax—50.

Obama: Well, listen—listen up. Now, let me—now, let me make sure that we are clear on, on the facts here. I would take your marginal rate back to what it was under Bill Clinton—

O'Reilly: Yeah, and that was 39.

Obama: And that was—you go back to 39.

O'Reilly: Right.

Obama: You can afford that. That's point number one. Well, you can't deny that you can afford it.

O'Reilly: Yes.

Obama: It's not gonna hurt you.

O'Reilly: I am not gonna deny that.

Obama: All right? In exchange, I am cutting taxes—for 95 percent of Americans. Ninety-five percent—

O'Reilly: Well, guess what? Well, that's class warfare—

Obama: It's not—95 percent—

O'Reilly: And—

Obama: —is not class warfare.

O'Reilly: Wait, wait, wait, wait, wait.

Obama: And I am saying that 95 percent of the American people are getting a tax break—three times the amount of tax relief under my plan than John McCain's. And that's not my statistic—

O'Reilly: Here, here is—

Obama: —that is from—

O'Reilly: Here is what I got—

Obama: —from independent analysts.

O'Reilly: And, and, and it's not all about me, believe me.

Obama: Go ahead.

O'Reilly: Twenty percent more revenue coming in under Bush than Clinton, all right? And he cuts taxes, people invest more. And he cuts the capital gains. And the government gets 20 percent more than under Clinton. You want to raise it back up—it doesn't make sense. Secondly—

Obama: Well—

O'Reilly: Secondly—

Obama: Okay, go ahead.

O'Reilly: The payroll tax—over to 50? You are gonna hike it to infinity—

Obama: I am not.

O'Reilly: What, what's the cap?

Obama: That's not true—

O'Reilly: What's the cap?

Obama: And all, all—

O'Reilly: Hold it! What's the cap?

Obama: [*Laughs.*] All I said— [*Laughs.*] All I said is that after—

O'Reilly: Yeah?

Obama: Right? Then we could raise the cap. Not—

O'Reilly: That we could, or we will?

Obama: What I have said is, is that if we have got a set of options to stabilize Social Security—which I think is important—and I think you do, too, because there are millions of seniors out there—

O'Reilly: I do. Right.

Obama: —who depend on it. And we have got a couple of options. We could raise the retirement age—and I just left— talking to a whole bunch of guys who have been working—

O'Reilly: Look, I have no beef on this—

Obama: All right. So you don't want to do that. Number—or number two, we could cut benefits. Try living on Social Security right now; that's no fun if you are a senior. Number three, we could just do nothing, in which case Social Security will be—

O'Reilly: So—

Obama: And let me finish—and let me finish my point, Bill. Uh, in the upcoming years, it's gonna be essentially, uh, a reduction in benefits. We could raise the payroll tax on everybody—

O'Reilly: Don't do that.

Obama: Of course.

O'Reilly: Don't do that.

Obama: But there is no free lunch.

O'Reilly: But what I—

Obama: So my only point is—

O'Reilly: No, there is a free lunch.

Obama: What is the free lunch?

O'Reilly: The free lunch is that—you are taking the wealthy American—the big earners, okay?

Obama: Okay.

O'Reilly: You are taking money away from them, and you are giving it to people who don't have. That's called "income redistribution." It's a socialist tenet.

Obama: No. Bill—

O'Reilly: Come on, you know that.

Obama: Bill, Bill—

O'Reilly: You went to Harvard—

Obama: Teddy Roosevelt supported the "progressive income tax." Uh, look—

O'Reilly: Not at the level you do.

Obama: Bill, well, here is my point—listen, you, you are—you are making it out like I am talking about going back to 70 percent marginal rates—

O'Reilly: You are above 50—

Obama: No, I am not.

O'Reilly: For me, you are.

Obama: No, I am not. What I have said is you go—you go up to 39, all right? That's what it was under Clinton—

O'Reilly: I am 39, and I am payroll-taxed.

Obama: But that—

O'Reilly: —until you decide I am not.

Obama: But, but, but potentially, we have got to explore a raise in the capital gains—

O'Reilly: No—

Obama: But I have made a commitment—

O'Reilly: I think it's "income redistribution."

Obama: Here, here is—here is, here is the—uh, here is the general point that I have got to make. Look, I don't like paying taxes. What, you think I like writing a check? Why would I like to write a check any more than you do?

O'Reilly: Because you love your country.

Obama: Uh. . . . What I believe is, is that there are certain things we have got to do. And we have got to help people who are . . . who have a tough time affording college, so they can benefit like we have. People are having a tough time. They don't have health care. People who are trying to figure out, uh, how they are going to pay the bills. And there are certain things we have got to do. Our infrastructure—you—look at what happened in Beijing. You go to the Olympics, and these folks are building. And we have got, uh, sewer lines that are crumbling—

O'Reilly: And—

Obama: And, and, and at, and at a certain point, we have got to pay for it. Now, I, I am not—I, I, I—

O'Reilly: But it is only the very few that are gonna pay for it, okay?

Obama: Right.

O'Reilly: You are, you are not across-the-boarding it. You are going—

Obama: But, but Bill—

O'Reilly: "I am taking from the rich."

Obama: [*Laughs.*]

O'Reilly: "And I am Robin Hood Obama—"

Obama: Bill, if, if, if—

O'Reilly: "—and I am giving it—"

Obama: All, all, all I am saying is—

O'Reilly: And then you want to raise corporate taxes—

Obama: All I, all I want—no, I don't. That's not true.

O'Reilly: You want—

Obama: All, all, all I want—

O'Reilly: You don't want to raise them? You don't want to raise corporate taxes?

Obama: All, all I want—all I am saying is—all I am saying is, is that, if we have got something that we have got to pay for— Now, George Bush—under George Bush, the, the debt has gone up $4 trillion, all right? So that's the credit card we have taken out—on our kids—from the Bank of China—that they are gonna have to pay for—

O'Reilly: The war on terror, though. Come on.

Obama: Well, no, no, no. That, that—that's not true. Uh, the, uh . . . that has to do—in part—with the Bush tax cuts, and no cuts in spending.

O'Reilly: No, it can't be, because the Bush tax cuts—

Obama: So—

O'Reilly: —generated more income.

Obama: No. No, no, no.

O'Reilly: The spending is out of control.

Obama: No. Well, uh, look, uh. . . . The Bush tax—or the, the Bush record—the numbers are—were there. Four trillion dollars. Now, we have got a choice. We can keep on just borrowing and dump it on our kids, that's option number one.

O'Reilly: Or we can take it from the wealthy, and give it to everybody else—

Obama: Bill, we could have an across-the-board tax cut—uh, or tax, uh, hikes, what you just talked about.

O'Reilly: Which is not "income redistribution"?

Obama: Bill, but the problem is, if I am sitting pretty, and you have got a waitress who is making minimum wage plus tips—and I can afford it and she can't—what's the big deal for me to say, "I am gonna pay a little bit more"? That is part of community—

O'Reilly: Let me answer your question.

Obama: That is part of what the—America has always been about is, is that we rise and fall together. And that, I think—

O'Reilly: And Americans give a tremendous amount—more than any in the world—to charity.

Obama: But—

O'Reilly: Let me give you one more—

Obama: All right.

O'Reilly: — and then we'll go on to, uh—

Obama: Right.

O'Reilly: —the next thing. Listen, if you raise the cap gains tax, that's going to inhibit investment. I won't buy as many stocks, and many many more people won't, okay?

Obama: If, if what—

O'Reilly: If you do that—

Obama: If we, if we went up, if we went up—

O'Reilly: —it's gonna, it's gonna come back to bite you, Senator.

Obama: If, if we went up to a prohibitive rate—you are right. But look, I—

O'Reilly: Thirty percent on it. That's Vegas, man. I am not going with those odds.

Obama: I, I—

O'Reilly: Fifteen, I'll pay. Not 30.

Obama: I, I, I didn't go there. Uh, I didn't say we would go that high. Well, let's say we go up to 20. I have talked to—

O'Reilly: Twenty is okay.

Obama: That, that—

O'Reilly: Not 25.

Obama: Okay. Well, there—well, you and I agree.

O'Reilly: All right. Good.

The most difficult part of researching this book has been trying to ascertain what will happen to America's economy under President Obama. Things are so shaky, so murky, so unpredictable that, like Afghanistan, just about anything could happen—with the exception of a tax cut for me.

Here's what we know for sure:

- Unemployment hovers around 10 percent despite massive government spending to stimulate the economy.

- Because of that spending, the new ObamaCare health system, and corporate bailouts, the United States now owes more than 13 trillion dollars.

- The *New York Times* and other Pinhead Far Left organizations demand even *more* government spending. Apparently, owing 13 trillion is not enough. Let's go for it! Let's get that up to 15 trillion.

- If President Obama is worried about this staggering debt, he is hiding it very well.

- Beginning on New Year's Day 2011, many, many taxes will rise in America. My federal income tax rate, for example, will go up to 39.6 percent. My payroll taxes will also go up. In fact, just about everything the feds can tax, they will tax. And all that additional revenue will not come even close to denting the deficit if the Obama administration continues its spending spree.

- Capital gains tax (the money you make when you sell profitable investments) will rise 5 percent to 20 percent, as Mr. Obama and I discussed.

- But interest on savings (yeah, sure, for many of us) will be taxed to the tune of almost 40 percent, a punishing situation.

- If you die in 2011 or beyond and leave more than a million in assets, the feds will take 55 percent of what you have over that amount. Thank you very much for expiring.

I could go on and on, but you get the picture. President Obama wants our money even though higher taxation might put the economy back into recession. Higher taxes often mean that folks spend less in our consumer-driven economy. President Reagan got us out of a nasty recession by cutting taxes. President Obama is doing just the opposite.

The real danger down the road is a Value Added Tax (VAT). Even though the President is playing the Alfred E. Neuman ("What, me worry?") card on government spending, his guys know there's a bad economic moon rising. The federal government is already almost broke; when ObamaCare finally kicks in, it could send us over the bankruptcy cliff.

So say hello to my little friend, the national sales tax. They do this in Europe to raise entitlement money so that workers can have eight weeks of paid vacation and call in sick every ten days. It does get chilly in Sweden, you know.

The VAT would be a promise-breaker for Mr. Obama, but he may have no choice. Remember, he said he would not raise taxes on Americans making $250,000 or less a year. But a national sales tax stings everybody. Read my lips: a VAT is a broken promise.

Of course, all this could change if the Democrats continue to lose public support. If Republicans regain control on Capitol Hill, as many observers believe likely, all of President Obama's programs and economic visions will be carefully scrutinized.

Finally, I understand it is my duty as a citizen to pay taxes, so I do pay them and try to keep the whining to a minimum. But many Americans are not as fortunate as I am. They are struggling to keep their homes, but high and rising property taxes are killing them. They want to send their kids to college, but every time they turn around, the government is keeping take-home pay away from them. There has to be a balance.

Obviously, President Obama wants to redistribute income to the poor. But by creating an entitlement society, he hurts the working class. So how is that fair? One group of Americans gets free stuff from the feds, while the other group has to struggle to pay its bills. Senior citizens should not be worrying about being evicted from their homes because they can no longer pay school and general property taxes. Young families should not have their paychecks gutted by an endless series of government tax levies. Enough is enough with the entitlement society stuff. America gives people opportunities and most of us do well. Those who don't or can't do deserve to be treated fairly but should not expect the rest of us to support them. The struggle between traditional self-reliance and the potential nanny state is the most divisive issue in America today.

O'Reilly: All right. I'm talking as an American now, not as a journalist.

Obama: Go ahead, go ahead.

O'Reilly: Okay? All right. So I don't know you. I never met you. This is the first time we've ever had a chat.

Obama: Right.

O'Reilly: Uh, actually, the second, when I pushed your guy out of the camera range.

Obama: [*Laughs.*]

O'Reilly: Remember that? Wasn't that fun?

Obama: Oh.

O'Reilly: He actually came over and, and, and said, he was very nice, we had, before the—

Obama: He said you were very nice as well.

O'Reilly: Um, I'm sitting there and I'm an American. I'm sitting there in, uh, Bismarck, North Dakota. I'm sitting there in Coral Springs, Florida.

Obama [*overlap*]: Right.

O'Reilly: And I'm seeing Reverend Wright, I'm seeing Father Pfleger, who thinks Louis Farrakhan's a great guy. I'm seeing Bernadette Dohrn and Bill Ayers, Weather Underground radicals, who don't think they bond enough. I'm seeing MoveOn.org, who says "Betray-Us." And I'm seeing you go to a Daily Kos convention, and this week Daily Kos came out and said that, um, Sarah Palin's Down syndrome baby was birthed by her fifteen-year-old, with no proof, that they put that on

PINHEADS AND PATRIOTS ✳ 223

there. And I'm going, Gee, that Barack Obama, he's got some pretty bad friends.

Obama: All right, well, let—

O'Reilly: Am I wrong?

Obama: You are wrong. Let, let, let's start from scratch. Number one, I know thousands of people, right? And so, understandably, people will pick out folks who they think they can criticize.

O'Reilly: I don't know anybody like that. And I know thousands of people.

Obama: No, no. No, no—

O'Reilly: I don't know anybody like that.

Obama: But, no, I, hold on a second, let, let me, let me make my point now. The, uh, the Wright thing we've talked about. But the, uh, I joined a church, to worship God, and not a pastor. This whole notion that he was my spiritual mentor and all this stuff, this is something that I've con—uh, consistently discussed. I had not heard him make the offensive comments that ended up being looped on this show constantly. And I was offended by them, and ultimately was—

O'Reilly: You'd never heard those comments.

Obama: I hadn't heard those comments.

O'Reilly: He was selling them in the lobby at the church.

Obama: What can I tell you?

O'Reilly: How many times, uh, did you go to church a month?

Obama: You know, I'd probably go twice a month.

O'Reilly: And he never said inflammatory stuff—

Obama: He didn't say, he didn't say stuff like that. All right? So, so—

O'Reilly: He said white people were bad.

Obama: No. What he said was racism was bad. And that—

O'Reilly: And not "White people are bad."

Obama: There, there was no, no doubt that what he said was, "Racism is bad." But here's, here's my point. I mean, we've gone over this.

O'Reilly: Okay.

Obama: The fact is, the relationship was ruptured, I'm not a member of the church.

O'Reilly: Right.

Obama: In both his case and Father Pfleger's case, they've done great work in the community, and I worked in some very poor communities. And the fact of the matter is, is that they've built senior housing, they provided day care, and those were the, that's how I got to know these folks, because I was working in these neighborhoods, where, you know, there's some good and there's some bad. All right? So that, that's on that point. Now, on this Ayers thing, which you, you've been hyping, Bill, pretty good.

O'Reilly: Not, not that much.

Obama: But, you know—but here, here, here's the bottom line.

O'Reilly: Yes.

Obama: This guy did something despicable forty years ago.

O'Reilly: He did something despicable last week—said he didn't do enough bombing. That's last week.

Obama [*overlap*]: What, what—I haven't seen the guy in a year and half, but he—

O'Reilly: But you know he's on the Woods Foundation board.

Obama: Let, let, let, let me make—

O'Reilly: You know who he is there.

Obama: Let me, let me finish my point, all right? Here's a guy that does something despicable when I'm eight years old.

O'Reilly: Okay.

Obama: All right? I come to Chicago. He's working with Mayor Richard Daly, not known to be a radical, right, on education issues, and he's a professor at the Department of Education, right?

Obama: Yeah.

O'Reilly: So he and I know each other, as a consequence of work he's doing on education. That is not an endorsement of his views. That's not—

O'Reilly: No, but you guys partnered up on a youth crime bill, remember that?

Obama: And it was a good bill.

O'Reilly: No, it wasn't. That bill said that if a youth commits a second violent felony, he does time in an adult prison. That's two shots. You, you said no. You knew the South Side of Chicago.

Obama: No. No, no, no.

O'Reilly: You know how many people are harmed.

Obama: No, but, but, but what happened with—listen, you're absolutely right. My community gets hit by crime more than any—

O'Reilly: And I'm right on that bill. You were wrong on that bill.

Obama: I disagree with you on that bill. But that's, that's a policy—

O'Reilly: You don't want to send—

Obama: No, no. Hold on. Hold on.

O'Reilly: —kids who are hurting other people away?

Obama: We're, we're, we're, we're getting, we're getting too far off field here.

O'Reilly: Oh, that's important, though. You, you and Ayers were allied on that bill.

Obama: No, no. Look, he didn't write that bill.

O'Reilly: Nah, he was supporting it. And so were you!

Obama: No. [*Laughs.*]

O'Reilly: But you guys were together on it.

Obama: No, no. Hold on a second. Now, now, now we're getting—

O'Reilly: All right, if that's unfair, I'm sorry.

Obama: That, that's pretty flimsy. Here, here's the point. All right? This guy is not part of my campaign, he's not someone—

O'Reilly: Well, he's, he's—

Obama: He's not some ad—he's not some adviser of mine. He is somebody who worked on education issues in Chicago, that I know.

O'Reilly: And you were on a board at the Woods Foundation.

Obama: Right. And, and, and, and who did something despicable forty years ago. But, but let me make the, let me make the broader point here, Bill. The problem that your viewers, your guys, your folks, the folks you champion, the problem you're going through, that, the problems they're going through, with trying to pay their bills, trying to keep their jobs, trying to move up in this world, their problem isn't Bill Ayers. It was Bill Ayers forty years ago, when he was blowing stuff up.

O'Reilly: They want a President, they want a President whom they can identify with.

Obama: They want a President that, that—

O'Reilly: They want a President that they can identify with.

Obama: And they, and they should be able to identify with me because my story is your story.

O'Reilly: But your associations are not my associations.

Obama: Your story, and the story—but, but—

O'Reilly: MoveOn, General Betray Us, the Daily Kos?

Obama: I was offended by that. And I, and I said, I was offended by it.

O'Reilly: But you, but you said good things about them. You showed up to the Kos convention.

Obama: But, but look, Bill. Bill.

O'Reilly: You don't get worse than these.

Obama: Bill. Hold on a second. I mean, there's a whole bunch of stuff, uh, said on Fox about me, that, that is [*chuckles*] flagrantly biased.

O'Reilly: Correct the record. Correct the record.

Obama: Well, but I still, I still don't mind coming on your show. Just because there are a whole bunch of things that may be said on this network that I completely disagree with, I don't sort of assume that you have to take responsibility for everything that is said on Fox News, any more than I would expect you to take responsibility for everything that's said on Daily Kos. Think about it. The, the—

O'Reilly: Well, the, that's a hateful thing. Fox News is not hateful.

Obama: No, they're not, they're, they're, they're— [*Laughs.*]

O'Reilly: Oh, it isn't. The, some of those guys—

Obama [*overlap*]: Bill. The—

O'Reilly: —Some of our commentators might think—

Obama [*overlap*]: If, if, if, if you were watching Sean Hannity consistently, you, you would—

O'Reilly: He's a commentator, though.

Obama: Well, that's all these bloggers are. I'm not making an excuse for 'em.

O'Reilly: Oh, whoa. Hannity's never said he wants—

Obama: They, they, they've gone—

O'Reilly: —Dick Cheney to die of cancer.

Obama: Hold on. Hold on, hold on, hold on a second. All I'm saying is, these guys, they're giving me a hard time. You know, one, one of the times they gave me a hard time—

O'Reilly: They're raising the kind of money for you . . . [*inaudible*]

Obama [*overlap*]: You know one of the times they gave me a hard time? Was when I went to campaign for Joe Lieberman. Now, Joe didn't mention that in his [*chuckles*] speech—

O'Reilly: They gave you a hard time about voting for the, uh—

Obama: So, so it's not, all I'm saying is, I expect to be held responsibile for the things I say and do. And one of the things that's happened in this campaign, and I think that you have the power to help correct the record on this, is not to put me in a position where every tangential relationship—

O'Reilly [*overlap*]: It is, it is a pattern of behavior here.

Obama: It, it, no, there, it is not a pattern of behavior. It is guilt, it is classic guilt by association. And—

O'Reilly [*overlap*]: The pattern of behavior is that you feel very comfortable, for some reason, in Far Left precincts. That's the pattern of behavior.

Obama: But I don't—

O'Reilly: That I see.

Obama: But I, Bill, I've got friends who are, who are on the Far Right.

O'Reilly: Who?

Obama: They're, I've got colleagues in the Senate.

O'Reilly: Who? Give me a name.

Obama: Well—

O'Reilly [*overlap*]: [*Laughs.*] I always do that.

Obama: Well, no, but, you know, but, but—

O'Reilly: I, I'm sorry, I didn't mean to embarrass you.

Obama: —but here's what happens, if I give a name, then people—

O'Reilly: [*Laughs.*]

Obama: —then the next thing I'll know is, people will say, "They're comparing this one to that one."

O'Reilly: Do you know what I wanted to hear?

Obama: " . . . To Bill Ayers, and I . . ."

O'Reilly: "I go hobnobbing with Rush Limbaugh." That's what I wanted to hear there.

At the risk of being redundant, let me give this "associations" deal another shot. If you are a dope dealer who sells heroin and cocaine, you are an evil person. You are hurting people, and you know that what you peddle can lead to addiction and even death. But you don't care.

On the other hand, if you sell marijuana, you might see yourself as benign, as someone just providing a service, a harmless enjoyment to those who seek it. But the truth is, if you are in the drug world, selling hard or soft drugs, you will be exposed to many bad things. There is no avoiding the pernicious associations that permeate that culture.

There is an analogy here. Barack Obama's entire career has been nurtured by liberal people. Some of them are mainstream, just folks who believe that government has a moral duty to help the downtrodden by creating mandates that require a huge government apparatus and trillions of taxpayer dollars.

But some of the people with whom Mr. Obama has associated in the past are far more than left-wing ideologues. They are extremists. The Reverend Jeremiah Wright and Bill Ayers are crazy guys, people consumed with hatred toward their own country.

Barack Obama should have avoided these men, but he did not. To him, they were part of the Chicago liberal culture that was supporting his rise to power. The question is: How much sympathy does the President have toward the extremist point of view?

The record shows that he has appointed some hard-core radical people like Van Jones to government offices. So I think it's safe to say that radical Left beliefs do not offend the President. The Daily Kos is fine with him. George Soros has visited him in the White House on many occasions.

Those facts indicate that the President of the United States has no problem with radical Left thinkers and believers. The evidence shows that he listens to what they have to say. Whether or not he buys into the Soros view of the world is a matter of conjecture. I don't think old Georgie would be dropping drone missiles on al-Qaeda terrorists, so that's something.

There's an old saying that applies here, however: If it walks like a duck and quacks like a duck, then it's Jeremiah Wright at the pulpit. Again, Mr. Obama claims that he just never knew how hateful and radical Wright really is.

Yeah, and I'm Whoopi Goldberg.

So let's cut through all the fog and clearly state the issue to be sure no one missed it the first time: President Obama is the most liberal chief executive ever to serve in the Oval Office.

Sorry, Jimmy Carter.

O'Reilly: All right, look, I got one more question that I forgot that's important.

Obama: Go ahead.

O'Reilly: A hundred and fifty billion to alternative energy in the Obama administration.

Obama: Yeah. Over ten years.

O'Reilly: Okay. Over ten years.

Obama: Yeah.

O'Reilly: To what? To what? What, don't, aren't, shouldn't we have a plan, before we start to spend?

Obama: Oh, no, no.

O'Reilly: Is it going to be ethanol? Is it going to be fuel cells?

Obama: Let, let, let, let, let me—

O'Reilly: What's it going to be?

Obama: Let, let, let me give you some examples. Uh, number one, uh, we have to extend tax credits for solar, wind, hydro, which is basically the hydro—

O'Reilly: But you're scattershotting it, though. What if, what if solar wind and hydro don't work?

Obama: No, no, no. No, no—but, but, but, but that, that was true for the space program. We didn't—

O'Reilly: Always focus on the space program.

Obama: Kennedy didn't know how we were going to go to the moon. That, that, the nature of discovery, and research, and innovation, is you put money into a whole bunch of promising pots. It's like venture capital. And you figure out what works. And some things are going to work, and some things are not. You're not going to bat a thousand. But here's what we know. We can't keep doing the same things we're doing. Look, I had a meeting with T. Boone Pickens.

O'Reilly [*overlap*]: I'm with you. I'm with you.

Obama: Here's an example. T. Boone, you know, did some things with, uh, respect to John Kerry and voting that I thought, uh—

O'Reilly: No, he's the wind guy now, and we, I'm with you on that.

Obama: —but he and I sat down and had a conversation because he is absolutely right, that we can't sustain importing 70 percent of our oil.

O'Reilly: Everybody knows that. But you've got to have a plan.

Obama: That's right. And I, I do have a plan.

O'Reilly: You should get nukes involved. Why are you against nuclear energy, when Sweden does it?

Obama: I am not—I am not against nuclear energy.

O'Reilly: Well, let's get the plants up!

Obama: Well, okay, why not?

O'Reilly: Let's start drilling in ANWR [the Arctic National Wildlife Refuge]. What are you going to—

Obama: Who's arguing with you?

O'Reilly: Are you afraid, are you afraid of scaring—

Obama: No. Now, ANWR, ANWR I think is a problem for us.

O'Reilly: What, a caribou is going to be scared?

Obama: [*Laughs.*]

O'Reilly: Come on!

Obama: [*Laughs.*]

O'Reilly: You, you're with the folks that complained about heating bills, and you're worried about a caribou going, "What's that pipe thing doing?"

Obama: No. But, but, I tell—

O'Reilly: What?? What??

Obama: One of the great things about this country is you travel around, is, you've got a, some beautiful real estate here.

O'Reilly: Oh come on. Nobody goes to ANWR.

Obama: We got, we got lots of, we—

O'Reilly: You know, what do you want to do, run shuttles up there?

Obama: We are lucky to have some of the most beautiful, uh, uh, real estate on earth. And we want to make sure that—

O'Reilly [*overlap*]: You're making me cry here.

Obama: We want to make sure we'll pass it on to the next generation, but this notion that I'm opposed to nuclear power, it's just not true. The notion that I am opposed to—

O'Reilly [*overlap*]: What I'd like to see—

Obama: —coal, is not true. What I have said is that we've got to invest in the technologies that make 'em cleaner.

O'Reilly: That's swell.

Obama: You and I agree on that.

O'Reilly: But what I'd like to see between now and election day—

Obama: All right.

O'Reilly: —and I think it would get you some votes, is say, Look, this is what I'm going to do.

Obama: Yeah.

O'Reilly: I want to hear, We're gonna, we're gonna get this many new plants.

Obama: Right.

O'Reilly: We're going to put this much into solar. We're going to get this, this, this. And that would drive down the price of oil.

Obama: I'll, I'll help you, uh, uh, I'll—

O'Reilly: No, that's your deal. I'm not running for anything.

Obama: No, no, no. I'll make sure to send that plan, so that you can start advertising it for us.

O'Reilly: Well, you can come back on and tell me.

Obama: I look forward to it.

> So am I a prophet or what? I pounded then-Senator Obama on his objections to drilling in ANWR and his lack of a specific vision for alternative energy, which the country desperately needs.
>
> Then, about a year and a half after that interview, BP befouls the Gulf of Mexico, forcing President Obama to address the nation and to promise to invest billions in nonspecific alternative energy projects. Yes, the President is consistent. No, he is not advancing the energy ball down the court. The United States still does not know how to replace oil.
>
> We could, however, replace deepwater drilling if we opened up ANWR. But the President will not alienate the environmental Left by doing that. I guess it's better to have pelicans and turtles covered with oil and the saltwater marshes of Louisiana turned into toxic garbage dumps. But, hey, should you care to visit, the Arctic Circle is spotless.

O'Reilly: All right, now. Final question for you. I think I can kick your butt in one-on-one basketball.

Obama: You've got height.

O'Reilly: Okay.

Obama [*overlap*]: But I think I've got speed.

O'Reilly: But you have, but you've got youth. I'm an old guy. I'm seventy-three years old.

Obama: Are you seventy-three?

O'Reilly [*overlap*]: Yeah, this is Botox.

Obama: Is that? You look good, man.

O'Reilly: How many are going to spot me on the—

Obama: What do you eat, to be looking like that at seventy-three?

O'Reilly: I don't, I don't eat anything.

Obama: [*Laughs.*]

O'Reilly: How many are you going to spot me on a one-on-one game, huh?

Obama: Uh. . .

O'Reilly: 'Cause I think I—

Obama: Game to eleven?

O'Reilly: Yeah.

Obama: I'd spot you ten.

O'Reilly: All right. You'd spot me ten. That's pretty cocky.

Obama: [*Chuckles.*]

O'Reilly: That's pretty cocky. So now I win, right, I want to be secretary of state.

Obama [*overlap*]: Now, now I hear you're, I hear you're—

O'Reilly: No, no. If I win, I want to be secretary of—

Obama: I hear you're, I hear you're a pretty good athlete, but, but your game was football and baseball, right?

O'Reilly: Right.

Obama: Different than basketball.

O'Reilly [*overlap*]: And I, I think I could—

Obama: But you do have height.

O'Reilly: But white guys can't jump. You know, I, I think Reverend Wright said that, didn't he?

Obama: I'm sure he did.

O'Reilly: Ha, ha, ha!

Obama: I think that was Bill O'Reilly.

O'Reilly: Senator, a pleasure.

Obama: I enjoyed it.

O'Reilly: I enjoyed it, too.

Obama: Thank you so much.

O'Reilly: I hope you come back.

Obama: We'll be back.

O'Reilly: And good luck in the campaign.

Obama: Thank you so much. Appreciate it.

So I snuck in that Reverend Jeremiah Wright jab. If you saw the interview on TV, you may have noticed that Mr. Obama's smile dimmed a bit upon hearing that. Some people hammered me for ending the chat with a bit of mindless banter, but I say, give me a break. I appreciated the opportunity to talk with the man and wanted to leave on an up note. After all, he didn't have to submit to the interview, which, by the way, could very well be the toughest one he's ever done.

Also, just as I did not dislike President Bush, I don't dislike President Obama. They are human. They do good things; they do bad things. Like all of us. I enjoy talking to these guys. They are both smart and have experienced incredible things. When I visit the White House for an interview, I am totally engaged. But that doesn't mean I'm starstruck. My main obligation is to you. I think my interviews with both Presidents demonstrate how I keep that in mind.

For me, things get complicated when a President's policies adversely affect you. President Bush let Iraq get out of control for a while and did not watch the Wall Street bandits closely enough. The brutal fallout from those failures hurt most Americans.

Right now, President Obama is spending the country into peril. In addition, his liberal view of the world has not resulted in any improvement in the lives of most of us. His big issue, ObamaCare, remains a wild card. Nobody knows how that will work out. What we do know is that it will be expensive and complicated.

Finally, we are now firmly in the age of Obama, a fact that has a direct effect on your life. He is dominating world events but has not delivered on the "hope" promise. "Change," yes.

In just a short time, the President has become a polarizing figure, who is most likely in over his head as chief executive of the most powerful country the world has ever known. But so were Abraham Lincoln and Ronald Reagan in the beginning of their White House tenures.

As for your place in this age? It's to assess the country and your personal situation honestly; it's also to be a loyal citizen no matter what your political and social allegiances.

As Mr. Obama's first term moves along, polls show that most Americans have lost some confidence in his ability to lead. The blunt truth is that most of us are not better off than we were in the last year of the Bush presidency, not exactly a shining moment for America.

But as my pal Billy Joel once sang, keep the faith. Throughout our gallant history, Americans have always responded to tough situations by fighting through them and electing great men and women to represent us. If President Obama does not institute policies that improve the lives of most Americans, he will be voted out in 2012. I have no doubt. The system will work.

In the meantime, he's a Patriot for serving his country but also a Pinhead on some important issues. We will know rather soon which label will override the other.

It's All About You

SO WHAT DO *YOU* THINK? Not about President Obama and his policies, but regarding your place in your country. After all, that is the subtitle of this book. How are you feeling these days about being an American? I'd sincerely like to know.

So if you would be kind enough to put together some thoughts and send them to O'Reilly@FoxNews.com, I will read them and highlight some of your musings on the Web site. Beginning in September 2010, we'll post daily updates written by everyday Americans about this book and about how folks perceive their own personal situations.

This will be fun and instructive. I want to know where you disagree me with me. If you see something in *Pinheads and Patriots* that strikes you the wrong way, let me hear it. I might even include some of your critiques in the paperback edition of this book. So let's get on it, people!

At the end of my books, I like to thank you, the reader. With all the options you guys have these days, it is a major compliment to me that you have taken the time to read what I have to say.

Also, I hope the book has given you some clarity about your life and the country in which you live. We are still the most prosperous, generous people on the planet, but things are changing rapidly in America, and your voice is important to steer that change in the right direction.

As you may know, I believe in the "power of the people." But, unlike the crazy radicals of the 1960s, I actually understand who "the people" really are. The folks to whom I speak are largely traditional-minded, fair, hardworking, and respectful of their country. They understand that it is not government that has made America great; rather, it is Mary and John, who live their lives honestly, fulfilling responsibilities no matter how difficult they may be. The power of change lies with those folks, and that is the great hope of the United States.

Things may not be the way we want them to be right now. Anger and discontent are in the air. But, always, the folks have prevailed and the nation has snapped back from hard times.

That will happen again. The people will rise and correct the political chaos that has taken place. That will happen for one very simple reason: in America, there are far more Patriots than Pinheads.

Bill O'Reilly
August 2010
Long Island, New York

CREDITS AND PERMISSIONS

★

p. 10   REUTERS
Photographed by Ho New

p. 15   Associated Press/AP
Photographed by Susan Walsh

p. 18   T-shirt Artwork by www.FreeSignArtwork.com

p. 21   Associated Press/AP
Photographed by Matt York

p. 26   Associated Press/AP
Photographed by Charles Dharapak

p. 36   Author's Collection

p. 41   Associated Press/AP
Photographed by Pool, Pat Lopez via WFAA

p. 44   Associated Press/AP
Photographed by Manuel Balce Ceneta

p. 52   Associated Press/AP
               Photographed by Cynthia Boll

p. 56   FreedomWorks

p. 58   Associated Press/AP
               Photographed by Scott Applewhite

p. 66   Associated Press/AP
               Photographed by Mary Altaffer

p. 73   Associated Press/AP
               Photographed by Manuel Balce Ceneta

p. 76   White House

p. 82   Author's Collection

p. 85   Reagan Library

p. 94   Associated Press/AP
               Photographed by Elise Amendola, File

p. 104   REUTERS
               Photographed by Shannon Stapleton

p. 106   Associated Press/AP
               Photographed by Paul Beaty

p. 112   Corbis Corporation
               Photographed by Shepard Sherbell

p. 124   Circle Newspaper, Marist College Archives

p. 137   Author's Collection
               Photographed by Ryan Eanes

p. 139   Author's Collection
               Photographed by Ryan Eanes

p. 141–42 Author's Collection
               Photographed by Ryan Eanes

p. 147   Author's Collection
               Photographed by Ryan Eanes

p. 152   Author's Collection
               Photographed by Ryan Eanes

p. 156   Author's Collection
               Photographed by Ryan Eanes

p. 160   Associated Press/AP
          Photographed by Jacky Zhao/Color China Photo/AP
          Images
p. 165   Associated Press/AP
          Photographed by James Pringle
p. 174   Associated Press/AP
          Photographed by Matt Sayles
p. 176   Associated Press/AP
          Photographed by Tammie Arroyo
p. 178   Associated Press/AP
          Photographed by Rene Macura
p. 179   Associated Press/AP
          Photographed by Mark Humphrey
p. 185   *The O'Reilly Factor*
p. 205   White House
          Photographed by Pete Souza

INDEX